Stupid Guy in the Midwest ®

Helpful Hints for Non-Custodial Dads and Stepmoms ®

iUniverse, Inc.

New York   Bloomington

iUniverse books may be ordered through booksellers or by contacting:

iUniverse
1663 Liberty Drive
Bloomington, IN 47403
www.iuniverse.com
1-800-Authors (1-800-288-4677)

Because of the dynamic nature of the Internet, any Web addresses or links contained in this book may have changed since publication and may no longer be valid. The views expressed in this work are solely those of the author and do not necessarily reflect the views of the publisher, and the publisher hereby disclaims any responsibility for them.

ISBN: 978-1-4502-6594-2 (sc)
ISBN: 978-1-4502-6595-9 (ebook)

Printed in the United States of America

iUniverse rev. date: 10/28/2010

Dedication:

This Book is dedicated to my loving wife, who is my rock as I continue to battle through these issues. To my deceased friend, Les, who gave me great advice as I was going through this HELL early on in my life and Jerry, who is like an uncle to me and walked me through a lot of the legal procedures.

Introduction:

This book came about as a type of therapy for me and as I wrote, I began to feel that there was more of a purpose to this than something I needed to do for me.

It is my hope that through this book, others will learn from my mistakes and get an upper hand that will help them prepare for a potentially challenging time ahead called "Divorce with minor children." I hope to help others see and more importantly, acknowledge the signs that can lead to a rather unfavorable and expensive outcome through the bias court systems that are far from just.

Through my trials, I have learned that "He or she who is the best actor or actress" wins the case. It is not about the kids, as the court system and child services tends to preach but about money; plain and simple. Continuation after continuation, the court systems are designed to be money machines for their jurisdiction. The signs or omens of what is to come are out there long before the papers are filed. We just need to open our eyes, ears and stop fooling ourselves into thinking that if we just ignore those signs, they will go away. Wake up, learn and prepare so that the misery I have gone through isn't in vain and you are prepared for a more favorable outcome than I was; for you and the sake of your children.

To understand how I ended up with Satan or "She who's name should not be mentioned," I must first explain a bit of my upbringing and the church we were raised in. Sit back, enjoy and learn from "The Stupid Guy in the Midwest."

My Childhood

As I reminisce on my life, I find it rather unbelievable. I was born a 3 pound preemie in Hades Town Ohio. The year was 1964. I'm lucky number seven and only nine months younger than my sister, Selene. My parents kept busy. I soon learned to fend for myself just to survive against my brothers, as many children who grow up with a lot of siblings learned to do. As the youngest in a household of limited means, my three older brothers would always try to take my food, so I would quickly eat to avoid losing the little I was rationed to those beasts. I soon learned to defend myself. I had 3 sisters. Betsy was the oldest girl who always took care of me. I was her favorite so she would care for me like a mother would her child. At the age of seven, I would pack my own school lunches of peanut butter and jelly and fend for myself in many ways.

I wore hand-me-downs to school which had gone through a bit of abuse after three boys. The wear and tear was apparent so they were embarrassing to wear. This motivated me to find work at seven years of age. I would do the typical childhood jobs to earn money around the neighborhood, like grass-mowing and raking. I did whatever I could do to earn money in order to buy decent clothes for school and whatever else I needed. I remember one year I bought a skateboard and my brother broke his hand while riding it down the driveway. My father made me get rid of it because of my brother's stupidity.

Much of my work ethics came from my upbringing so it wasn't all a waste. In my house, we grew our own vegetables, which prepared us for long hours of labor in the back yard, gardening and weeding. As a child, I hated that garden! It did however, help instill my solid work ethics and endurence. Every Sunday we worked from 9am until 7pm, weeding or shoveling horse manure from the local racetrack, for the garden. Let me tell you about the horse shit! My brother, my sister and I would have to get up to the top of the shit heap in the truck and stomp it down with our feet while my other brothers were shoveling it into the enclosed bed of the truck and laughing while they slung it at me. You have no idea how bad shit really smells until you're covered in it, in a low ventilated space. I was living the dream! Then we would take the manure home and unload it; dropping it by hand between the garden rows of food.

Although my family was pretty unusual, they were still more normal than many of the families in the neighborhood that had more than seven children. In fact, we were one of the smaller families in the neighborhood. I can write a book on the neighborhood alone.

Up until the age of seven, we would celebrate holidays with other family members. There would be great parties, an excess of foods, which wasn't common in my home, and a lot of socializing and participation with cousins and other extended family members. It was nice and as a child, I felt like I was special to be part of such a big family unit that did so much together.

My family celebrated Christmas until my parents became members of a church in our community. That's when all the family celebrations and reunions came to an end. The sect, who still exists today, is somewhat of a blend between Jehovah Witness, Seventh Day Adventists and Judaism. The church frowned on the celebration of Christmas, Easter, Halloween and birthdays, however, they would celebrate Thanksgiving and they would have the Feast of Tabernacle. In my eyes, it's nothing short of a cult. They focused and contemplated the end of the world. When the end didn't come on the proclaimed date then they would use an excuse that the calculations were off or some miracle occurred that extended their salvation. I remember living through at least three Ends of the World events; in the 80s, 90s and finally, The Year 2000. Yet, "We're still here!" Despite my resentment and outright dislike for this church, it has been good for my parents in many ways. Most of my siblings walked away with repercussions of some kind.

My parents were unconcerned about our grades. My grades suffered because I put little effort into the school curriculum; however, I always managed to do well on finals. This left my teachers suspicious so they would accuse me of cheating and I'd have to explain that I studied just enough to pass the grade. They knew I had potential but just didn't apply myself unless I had to. I was considered a trouble maker in school.

I did excel in sports and enjoyed it because I could take my aggressions out. I ran track, wrestled, and weight-lifted. I also played football and baseball but my parents would never show up or care about any of the sporting events I was involved in because the school was "worldly" and only the church mattered. I was an all-star player and would win most competitions because when I played, it was do or die. I gave it my all for the sense of accomplishment and self-fulfillment. My coaches at school begged my parents to allow me to play sports on Saturday, which is their Sabbath, but my father the Deacon would just say that it was against our religion to play on the Friday after sundown and on the Sabbath. My father would blow a head gasket because I wasn't home reading the bible and praying like the rest of them. That only helped fuel my growing resentment against religion in general.

Because of my abilities on the field, I was popular and enjoyed the attention that was given me, especially from the opposite sex. In high school, I got involved with pot and experimented with other narcotics. Hell. Why not? We were just waiting for the end of the world anyway. When my friends and I went out, we would cause such a ruckus at the football and baseball games that we'd be forced to leave. I enjoyed being bad and going against the grain. It's what I lived for!

My Worst Nightmare:

Now is when my true hell began, which we'll refer to as "Satan," my future ex-wife. Her parents were also part of the church cult and as the girls in the cult went, Satan was the most attractive but she was also an absolute and total bitch. Her personality hasn't improved to this day. Later in life, after many years of travel to different parts of the country, I realized that Satan was simply average in appearance compared to all of the beautiful, diverse women this world has to offer; but in my teen years and only knowing what was available in my backyard, this was all I knew at the time. Further on in life is when I would discover how badly my parents' church and Satan would affect my life.

As a part of this congregation, we were only allowed to associate with people from the church so after-school functions became unacceptable. Satan attended a different high school than I did but we began dating. She was a cheerleader for her school team but since some of the games took place on the Sabbath, she eventually quit cheerleading for her high school and instead became a cheerleader for the church games. Satan would laugh at all the other cheerleaders because she was a "Professional High School Cheerleader" compared to these girls. She was the typical blonde that thought she was something more than what she was, but like I said, if she was the prettiest and in essence "average" you can just imagine what the others looked like.

I was the bad boy type, trying to go against the church at every opportunity. Even as a young boy, I couldn't fit into their system;

I was always in trouble. The Deacons and Church Officials would check me at the door and send me home if I didn't wear a suit and tie to church or if I refused to subject myself to their controlling ways. I was on their "watch" list and marked as a trouble-maker. I refused to be baptized so I was not fully accepted by the members, luckily, my ego was greater than their rejection of me.

Satan's "Wonderful" Family Life:

Before Satan and I dated, at her ripe age of fifteen, many of the church members attended a church convention in Florida, which included her family and mine. Satan would sneak out to drink until she was so intoxicated she could hardly stand. She flirted and made out with all the guys, or rather, they made out all over her. One of the guys in particular was a very close family friend. She had no boundaries. I was unfortunately absent from the event and very disappointed not to be involved in the "group activity" she had provided, but the other guys made sure to tell me about it the following day. Upon her return to the hotel, her father was in a rage and would beat her with his belt for her behavior. Her mother and sisters would be present to watch as he beat her so that she became the example for her other sisters, should they attempt to behave in that whorish manner.

Satan's father was the church Deacon and Treasurer and due to their constant overspending and always living above their true meager means, he would use the church funds to pay their personal debts. The truth would come out during dinner. Her father would brag about his misuse of church funds and how stupid they were not to discover his activities and account doctoring. He would justify it by saying that it was ok because he would replace it and no one would be the wiser. Who knows if he really did since they were always behind financially. I seriously have my doubts, knowing his character.

Her father would constantly brag about how "smart" he was, which also provided another indication of his true colors. Back in the 80s, before satellite tv, he got his hands on an illegal cable TV box so he could install it and pick up free cable. This went on for seven years until he got caught by the cable company. Satan would tell me how her father would close everyone's bedroom door on Friday night since they had to go to bed early for church the next morning. He would then say that he was going to stay up and read the bible but instead he'd sit in the family room and watch porn. "Do as I say; not as I do."

Going out to dinner with her family was another adventure. As if listening to them question the waitress about everything on the menu wasn't bad enough, they needed to be certain that the food didn't contain any "unclean" pork or gill-less fish because it was a sin to eat it; Satan and her father would complain about the quality of their food in order to get a free meal. They behaved as if they were high society and would degrade the servers. Satan carried many of her father's traits and behaviors into her adulthood. If her father could sue someone to make a buck, he would and usually did, even if the person was a church member in their congregation. The man carried a lot of anger in his life that stemmed from his own childhood, just like Satan. I distinctly remember that her father also complained about being the middle child and having much of the same stigma she carries. Did I mention how righteous they were? I'm sure at this point you have a good indication of their character. Satan's grandparents had a small pension and when they passed away the family fought for the money. Her father would complain about what his brothers were given by his parents over the years. Satan's grandparents were also against the church so they stayed away from her family, preferring to visit their other sons instead. Her father was not much different from his father and she has inherited the same negative attributes and insecurities.

I was seventeen when we began dating and Satan was sixteen. She would tell me how ashamed she was of her parents and her home. She never wanted her friends to come visit her at home because she thought it was small and beneath her standards. Her father was very abusive, both physically and verbally. He was always screaming from the top of his lungs at the family for the most minuet things. I guess this is where she learned to do the same. Like father; like daughter. Her father would scream and belittle her mother if the supper wasn't on the table at exactly 4:00 pm. He would scream and degrade her if the potatoes were lumpy and the butter wasn't on the table or the bread was missing. There was always something wrong in her dad's eyes at dinner time, and he would carry on like a mad man. It was a madhouse but don't feel bad for Mommy Dearest because she talked about everyone behind their back. Such a kindly individual she was. Now when her dad grilled steak, he would burn it on many occasions but no one was allowed to complain. He always behaved as if he could do no wrong. Daddy Dearest was always trying to be the center of attention, especially during church functions. He was very much the brown noser. A more negative soul didn't exist until Satan came into the world and the competition between them is very close, I might add.

Satan had a major hang up about being the middle child. She felt that she wasn't treated fairly by either parent. In her eyes, she never got enough attention and would buy books related to the middle child syndrome. Satan was jealous of her younger sister. There was a constant war raging between all the members of that family. Everyone in that family always had a problem of some kind. The controversy and issues were rampant. I doubt anything has changed to this day. Her family life made mine sound like a picnic but if you heard her and her family at trial, one would think that she came from a perfect family unit. Here is where acting lessons can really pay off.

I can't remember how I proposed to The Devil. It was just one of many bad memories I suppressed. I do remember that once we were engaged, I still wasn't allowed to sit in the same room with her alone and to top it off, she was 19 at the time. Both her parents would check her from top to bottom and smell her breath for alcohol since I was known for partying. One night, she arrived home a little later than usual. The following day she told me that her father was waiting for her and began screaming while he threw her on her bedroom floor, then climbed on her while she kicked and screamed for help but no one helped her or did anything about it. Her father was over 225 pounds and she was a small framed girl of maybe 100 lbs.

When she told me about the incident, I wanted to kick the living crap out of him. In hindsight, I should have kicked her instead and kept on walking, but I was stupid; as if the incident with the guys, when she was fifteen, wasn't indication enough for the future.

I guess what attracted me to Satan back then was her defiant attitude. She was always in trouble for one reason or another. I should have taken that as a sign and ran like hell the other way but as the saying goes, "If I knew then what I know now." Live and learn, I suppose.

Satan would complain and cry about how her father didn't love her because she was a girl and the middle child. She just had so many hang ups! Like her father, she cheated and mistreated those around her. Her entire family had the "Holier than thou, I'm better than you" attitude.

My sister Selene was a friend of Satan's, when they were teenagers and before I ever met the bitch. During a visit from my sisters in May 2009, we were discussing book and Selene commented that although she didn't really see that nasty side of Satan with our family, mostly because Selene later married and moved out of state, she did remember listening to Satan bad mouth other people and do nasty things to those around her. NOW, she tells me! But, I would have likely not listened back then anyway. Lust is blind. As I mentioned, she was the prettier of the bunch and I was vain.

Her Sisters:

After we were married, through the years, more of her family secrets emerged. Satan then confided in me that one of her sisters had told her about an affair their father had, which resulted in another child he never acknowledged.

Satan's sisters weren't much better. To begin with, the youngest one got kicked out of church because she was caught having sex in Indianapolis with another church boy. She already had a reputation for being a slut but the parents always denied it, yet this sister also lived with yet another church boyfriend for three years under her parent's roof before they were married. Her parents behaved as if nothing ever happened while the couple lived under their roof in sin. They merely slept together on the same bed, but there were no sexual relations. Yeah right!! Every time we visited, her younger loose sister and the boyfriend were in their night clothes. That family justified everything they did in their weird twisted minds. So after her sister finally married, she then began to date her future "second" husband and another older man she met while working at a strip club. During this time, she was still married to the first guy. The younger sister and her first husband had a son and a daughter together during their approximate five year marriage.

They began plotting against the first husband in preparation for the divorce by telling stories at dinner time about how he liked to have weird sex, using a carrot and different vegetables. Her sister would mention how her soon-to-be-ex would touch their children inappropriately. All I could think of was that the guy was a freak!

Every week they would add a little more to the story. Her parents would begin to degrade his parents and the man they allowed to live in their home, with their daughter for three years before he was married to her, by stating that his mother would still give his thirteen year old brother baths. These stories would be spread throughout their church as the stories only became more radical and twisted. Remember this, as it will make more sense later.

Satan's older sister, Johnny, is a lesbian and when she was a child, Daddy Dearest would buy Johnny cars and guns to play with instead of dolls. I guess if he couldn't create a boy, he'd turn one into a boy. Yet, in the eyes of the church, they were model parents but as soon as they returned home, their true colors would be revealed and hell would begin anew.

Wedded Bliss-ter:

In my early years, I worked as a mechanic but I wasn't making enough money, so I became a roofer, which paid a little better but it was back-breaking work.

Despite my parents' objections, I married my Nightmare in 1985, at the ripe and very viral age of 20. If there was ever a good time to listen to my parents, this was it. But nooo, I knew better. Her parents and mine were good friends but my parents knew that she wouldn't be right for me.

I should have known things were not going to be "Happily ever after" when I spent my wedding night with my friends, drinking and partying, while she was running around trying to get noticed. She was eating up the attention. No sex that night but I sure had a good time without her. It should have stayed that way.

Shortly after the wedding, we finally rented a house. Our relationship was never what an ideal marriage should be, but based on my buddies' marriages, I thought that's how it was supposed to be. I was too stupid to realize that she was unfaithful and that marriage was supposed to be something more than what mine was or those of my friends'.

Satan always wanted more. Nothing I did was enough for her. She had higher standards and thought she was high society on a McDonald's budget. Her father was an engineer making $40k a year so they thought highly of themselves. They were always in heavy debt and couldn't save money to save their own lives. She followed the "Spend" mold her parents lived by. Her behavior is practically identical to her father's. The one man she loved and hated.

At the beginning of our marriage, I would become jealous and upset if another man looked at her but as time passed, I started to see it more as a compliment to her. She always enjoyed the attention and would go out of her way to become the center of admiration. Again, we're talking about Ohio. Many of the women there are pretty generic in appearance, although in time, I found some to be prettier as they aged; it's certainly not a diverse part of the world like Florida is. The women there were mostly blondes, with fine features and small or no lips. Satan would complain about being flat in certain regions of her body where other women were more voluptuous; she was just small and slender with few curves and no hips.

Time just moved on and I tried to focus on other ventures, leaving her to her own devices and insecurities.

The Career Switch:

One day, while I was working up on a roof at a breaking temperature of 120 degrees and sweating like a pig, with blood seeping through my socks from my feet, I saw a guy in a black BMW pass by and thought to myself, "I know I can do whatever job he's doing." I had no idea what he did but I knew that I was motivated and capable, so in my determination to achieve success and a better life for my family of two, at the time, I decided to attend a local college downtown where I obtained an Associates' Degree in Computer Technology.

Shortly after graduation, I got my first gig as a Computer Programmer/Operator. I resigned after a couple of years due to the lack of pay and began working at a leasing company as a Computer Programmer, which is where I learned Synon. From then on, I worked as a Self-Employed Consultant for a variety of clients over the years. After a time, Satan complained that I wasn't home enough, so in an effort to appease her, I decided to try my hand at a fulltime local position for a consulting company. But Satan wanted more than I was able to provide as a full timer; $80k a year just wasn't enough for her, so I gave my two week notice and began working for SYNON, which is when the money really started rolling in.

As a Computer Consultant, the career required constant travel to client sites, which was usually out of state. It was stressful and very demanding. If things didn't go right, Consultants are always expendable.

I would either fly or drive out for work on Sunday night and return home sometime on Friday. Satan wanted a certain standard of living and it made me feel good that I could provide it. Unfortunately, sometimes one gives up their personal life in order to achieve success. Living out of hotel rooms and a suitcase became the norm. It wasn't so bad at first because I got to travel and experience things I would have never been able to experience otherwise.

Satan's Whor-ific Career and our life:

In 1987, Satan was hired in a law firm and a couple of years into the marriage she began having affairs with her married boss, who was one of the attorneys in the law firm. I actually accused her several times because I felt something wasn't right, but she denied it and I would foolishly believe her or was too busy with my career to give it much thought.

She would tell me that the Silver Fox, (which was the nickname a particular attorney from New York was given by the girls in the office) wanted to take her to the race tracks and then they would have lunch. I would just comment, "Well, It's a free day off of work." In hindsight, she was really "working" all her bosses over.

Then there were the bars and the after-work night caps. I love to drink and socialize and since she was always getting freebees, I wondered why I couldn't escort her to these events. There was always an excuse why I shouldn't be there. Then there were the weekends she'd get all dolled up just to work with her boss. I thought she was stupid for working the weekends. When I noticed her attire, she would reply that she liked to dress up but when I mentioned that she never dressed up for me, she would get angry and walk out.

Since she was spending so much time "working" and it was early in the marriage, I would ask her "Can't we have a weekend together and have sex?" I've always been a rather blunt person. Satan's reply was that we needed the money. I never did see her paycheck though. Yes, "What a moron I was!" This went on for years and I adapted to coming home and spending that time playing softball with my best friends, Les, Danny and the other guys from the church. We were always in trouble. It was great!

Some of these so-called "church" friends would come by my home to visit her while I was away. Upon my return, I'd find one of them in my apartment "alone" with Satan. It was a different male "friend" at any given time. I really never thought anything of it, because in my mind, they were just good friends visiting and checking up on her. RIGHT! What's the name of this book? You got it!

Satan came home devastated one day. She was crying because an attorney from her law firm had insulted her by loudly commenting, "You're nothing but a whore because you screw all the guys in the office!"

When she told me about it, all I could think of was kicking his ass. I don't know why I didn't bother to wonder why he would say that in the first place. By now, you could just imagine what kind of reputation she had. Men talk amongst themselves and office gossip tends to get around among the coworkers. She wasn't well liked.

Satan was finally fired from the law firm shortly after the "whore" incident with that attorney. The other women at the firm were happy to see her leave. She never got along with anyone because of her negative attitude and demeanor towards others.

Her lover/boss, whom we'll refer to as "Mr. Legal Eagle", made Partner in that firm. Shortly after that, Mr. Legal Eagle moved to Florida to work for another law firm, along with the attorney that called her a whore.

Our marriage was pretty mundane, so it was more of a relief to leave town for work, yet, I longed for a normal family life. Too much traveling can get old fast but every time I returned home, she would bitch about something or another. I think it was her way of keeping me at bay, especially since she was already having affairs by this time. I began spending more time away from home to avoid arguments and focus on the demands of the job. It got to the point that I would go home every two weeks instead. She still complained that I wasn't making enough money, even though I was making six figures, more than she could have ever made or hoped for on her own. I would eat dinner out of a can in my hotel room in order to avoid extra spending since she kept complaining about our debit; yet, my brother, Mark would see her enjoying and spending money at restaurants while I was away. This existence continued on for several years.

After being fired from her ex-lover's law firm, she went to work for a lesbian attorney at yet another law firm. She didn't like that her boss was a lesbian. Satan hated the woman because her boss required that Satan have a glass of coffee waiting on her desk every morning. In the afternoon, her boss wanted Satan to fill her glass with water, but Satan felt that she was too good to be a go-for girl. Satan filled the glass with water from the toilet and served it to her boss.

Satan would complain about the female coworkers having affairs with their male bosses, if that wasn't the pot calling the kettle black! After a few months at that firm, she was once again fired.

I was offered a job in Miami Florida and had fallen in love with that lifestyle long before the job came about. I loved the climate, so it was not a hardship to leave the Midwest behind. She was also trying to secure a position with Mr. Legal Eagle's firm, so we flew down on his dime.

It was still only the two of us. While in South Florida, Satan would dress up and go to lunch AND dinner with her ex-boss, leaving me at the hotel alone. I would go to the bar by the pool to kill time and enjoy the ambiance. My sister, Betsy, lived in South Florida so I'd call her and she'd join me for company.

During this time, Satan and I looked at houses in preparation for our move but wouldn't you know it, as soon as we returned home, Satan discovered she was pregnant with our first son. We were seven years into this miserable marriage and we were going to have a baby. By this time we were only having sex once every three months at best. Satan would comment that she thought I was sterile. Of course, I told her that since we rarely had sex, I WAS sterile. I would tell her that I should pickle my dick because that way it would be brand new when I pulled it out and really got to use it. That would infuriate her. Needless to say, she could not possibly be the one that was sterile because, after all, she was as flawless as her father. It was always someone else's fault.

After the discovery of her condition, Satan decided that she didn't want to move to Florida so she could be near her parents. Her parents! I didn't quite get it since she never had a good relationship with them in the first place, but I sadly turned down that great opportunity and continued my existence in the good ole Midwest.

Satan was then hired at a medical distribution company. Since she knew she was pregnant it was mostly for insurance purposes that she worked, however, she kept it hidden at first. I had a friend, Danny, that worked there so he helped get her the job since he was buddies with the owner, but that didn't stop her from bragging to her new coworkers how she was having an affair on me with her ex-boss, Mr. Legal Eagle. The women hated her. They were disgusted and appalled because this place wasn't the same kind of environment as the law firms where everyone was having an affair of sorts. Some of these women would disclose this information to my friend.

She would also complain to me how her current boss was having an affair with Satan's own assistant and she didn't like that. In hindsight, she was probably jealous because she really thought that she could have any man she wanted and when the advances weren't being made at her, but instead with another woman, it appears she would display disgust over the situation.

Now, although my friend Danny, found out about the affair Satan was having with Mr. Legal Eagle, he didn't say anything. He and his wife discussed it and thought I would "shoot the messenger" since my blinders were on so tight and he just couldn't bring himself to say anything because we were also expecting our first baby. He didn't want to be the cause of a separation between us; so instead, he kept quiet for eight years and hoped that Satan would settle down after the baby was born and be a proper mother and wife, which obviously never happened. I only discovered this truth later on during my separation from her. I was crushed and even though I had my suspicions, I'd put it out of my mind because I didn't want it to be true, but we'll get to that later.

Satan worked at the medical distribution company for eight months before she was fired. Again, the staff was happy and relieved to see her leave.

The New Additions:

We bought our first house shortly before the birth of my son, Sam. He was born in September of 1992.

During this time frame, Mr. Legal Eagle would fly back and forth from Florida to Ohio. I would be working out of town and she would notify me how they would have lunch and spend time together "reminiscing" about old times. By this time, I was more focused on work and she was hardly a concern anymore. Too many wasted years and a dysfunctional marriage does that to a person.

A couple of years later, my second son, Jack, came along. By this time, we were only having crappy sex once a year so I'm still not too sure how the second one happened! Jack doesn't look like me, but to her dismay, he has fragments of my personality. I'd come home, we'd fight and I would go off and have a few drinks. Then, I'd go to bed by myself.

When she conceived Jack, I remember her telling me that Mr. Legal Eagle was in town that week but I didn't think anything of it or really cared much at this point. Then, totally out of character, after I had fallen asleep, Satan would come into the room and initiate sex. She likely did this in the event that she might be pregnant, which was the case.

The boys gave me something to look forward to when I came home. They were my joy and we loved spending that time together. It was fun playing with them, watching them grow as they became aware of the world around them. I enjoyed experiencing those moments with them. They were my life. They were really all I had.

We would vacation in South Florida. I loved spending time at the beach and visiting with my sister, Betsy. While we were there, Satan would continue her rendezvous with Mr. Legal Eagle. They would spend the day together while I stayed with my two boys at the hotel. We'd spend the time swimming and enjoying the sun. My sister would visit us later in the day.

The back and forth, long distance affair between them continued throughout the years. We would visit Florida and Mr. Legal Eagle would visit the Midwest, always making sure to take her out for old times' sake. She must have put on a good show because she was a dead fish throughout our relationship or it was just free, easy and convenient for him. Even though, he likely had other women on the side.

Onward and Upward:

I was making six figures so she chose to become a Stay-at-Home mom and raise the kids. She was a failure in the work place anyway, so why go back to work just to continue being fired? Satan felt that we needed a larger home so we decided to have a brand new, 4000 square foot luxury house built to her specifications in the Paxton Lakes area. She thought she was royalty and wanted the best. The supervisors for Zaring Home Builders said that she was the most difficult person they had ever had the misfortune of dealing with. In other words, a total pain in the ass and complete Bitch! Anytime I suggested a preference in the house, she shot it down. Our tastes were as different as we were. We were total opposites and we couldn't even find a way to complement each other in any way.

My brief time at home would be spent with my two boys. After I tucked them in their beds, I would go into another room and get drunk with my brother Mark, where I would pity myself and my pathetic life. Being celibate made me upset and frustrated. On many occasions, I would tell her that I was going to pickle my dick so when I found someone that wanted it, it would still be new. And that would be the start of yet another fight. I would sleep in the playroom, near the boys. (Remember this part for later.) Then in the morning, I'd fly out for work, without any intimacy from her.

Now think about it. How would you feel if you came home, received no attention, no sex and the only thing you had to look forward to was a screaming match with a crazy bitch? Sounds like fun, huh? That was my life.

The visits with Mr. Legal Eagle continued on a regular basis, flying back and forth for business, and they would just so happen to have "lunch" every time. Of course I was out of town since I traveled to jobsites and she would always tell me "You would never guess who stopped by and we spent the day together." Did I get a clue? Of course not!! I was too stupid!!! You would think I would wake up and smell the shit being thrown at me, like those years of shoveling the stuff for the family garden, but I was too wrapped up in my work and travel because there was no time to deal with anything else. My weekends were limited and strictly for the boys at this point. I was always hoping things would change, but then, what's the definition of insanity? MY LIFE. Doing the same thing over and over again but expecting different results.

While the big house was being built, we discovered she was pregnant with the third child. She was absolutely furious about it. Mr. Legal Eagle had come into town that weekend she had conceived. She initiated sex with me, after seeing her lover, like she did when the second child, Jack, was conceived. Two weeks later she angrily showed me the test result and slapped me in the face over the positive outcome. This time, she should have slapped her lover instead.

Satan was a dead fish in bed but sex was sex. She always made a point to complain nonstop during the act. Yeah, that's a turn on!! BUT Hell! If you got it once a year, you're bound to end quickly. I was just too stupid to have my own affairs, which is something I should have done but it didn't occur to me because I WAS MARRIED.

Then again, it's the one thing she really couldn't use against me in court since she couldn't prove it. By the way, she did try to have me compromised but that's later on in the story.

We finally moved into the house and purchased expensive furniture along with a leased Lincoln Navigator for Her Highness. Baby Don was born and life continued into the state of mind called Hell. I thought Baby Don was mine until later when word of her affairs was made more public, during the separation. She denies the affairs to this day, but too many people know the truth because she likes to brag just like Daddy Dearest would do when he wanted to show people his intelligence. Let them talk and in time, they do themselves in.

While out of town, I'd call the house and my brother, Mark, would answer the phone. He'd be there doing jobs for me, such as cutting the grass, since my time at home was so short. I would gratefully pay him for his help. Mark was a fun uncle and the boys loved being with him. He never married nor had kids so they were like his own and he enjoyed his time with them. Mark would answer the phone and tell Satan I wanted to talk with her. He'd witness the scowl on her pale face every time she had to speak with me. He witnessed a lot since he was around quite often, including how she screamed at me and the kids all the time, her negative comments about me and those miserable looks. When we moved into the new house, I stopped subjecting myself to her abuse and finally began yelling back.

My brother, Mark, would be the one to pick me up from the airport because Mrs. "I-Don't-Have-A-Job" couldn't find the time to pick me up. She would get rid of the house keepers because they were never good enough for her. She'd bitch and moan about how hard her life was, even though she did nothing around the house, DIDN'T WORK and she found the boys to be nothing but trouble. So I'd get home to a messy house which I'd have the honor of cleaning during my limited weekends home. I couldn't figure out what the hell the woman did all day. I would have to clean the damn house every Friday night, usually finishing around 10pm, while Satan did nothing. Then she would just go to bed and not even thank me for helping, after I was away from home all week long. During this time, the boys would be in the playroom and I would also give the boys a bath and prepare them for bed because their mother was just too tired from her hectic week. Again, remember this part, it's important because it will all add up later.

Now, I'm not saying I'm a saint; my motive for cleaning the house was in the hopes of getting "lucky" which never happened. I thought that if I helped, she would be grateful and intimacy might follow. Lousy sex was better than no sex at this point. It never happened. Did I mention what the definition of insanity is?

My life consisted of flying out for work, living out of a hotel room unless I got to room with someone I knew, and eating food out of cans because although I made a six figure salary, we just never seemed to have enough money. Where was the money going? I would pay off the large credit card balances just to see them racked up again. I wasn't the one racking them up either.

One evening, we attended her high school reunion and I was placed at a table far off to the back because there was an old schoolmate she wanted to hook up with and since she never got the chance back then, maybe she'd get lucky now. They spent the night dancing while I socialized with other people. This guy was crying to her about his pregnant wife. By the following week, she would tell me "You'll never guess who I ran into?" I really didn't care at this point. I think I went from just stupid to neglectful where she was concerned since life with her was sheer misery. I only hung on for the sake of the kids at this point.

Later I discovered that she had called him all week on her cell phone and corresponded via email. I was home that weekend and babysitting while she was decked out to go to the toy store for four hours. The toy store happened to be beside a Holiday Inn. When she got home, I confronted her and she slapped me for accusing her of being unfaithful.

This was the inertia of my life in a nutshell. Come home every two weekends, spend them with the kids and no wife in sight, and then fly out alone all over again. When I would call Satan, sometimes one of her friends would answer the phone and sound nervous, asking me where I was. Satan never bothered calling me. When I did speak with her, she would say I was harassing her with so many phone calls. Our marriage, if it could be called that, lasted sixteen miserable years. Why do we do this to ourselves? Is a miserable known existence really better than the unknown? Why live in misery when we can likely live happier alone? I don't know, but most of us hang on to our lousy married lives rather than having to start over and battle the unknown single life all over again. People really don't want change until there's no choice; even if it would be better for them. All I can say now is that her decision to divorce me was the best gift I've ever received from her.

The court system in the Midwest is known for their ultra conservative mindset and that justice is not necessarily their true motive. A man walking into court is guilty until proven innocent! Here's where you guys need to start taking notes!

Watch for the Signs before you crash and burn:

Prior to receiving my divorce papers, we would always have holiday and dinner parties. At the time, I was working in Arizona and eating dinner out of a can. There was a woman I worked with who felt sorry for me and she knew I was going through a lot of stress being away from home and the boys. She had asked me if I would like to stay at her and her partner's house. I agreed because it was a money saving opportunity.

We held an extended family gathering on one of my weekends back home. Les, who was 20 years my senior and one of my best friends, had a daughter who was very much like Satan and she happened to be Satan's best friend. Misery loves company. She saw me in the kitchen and asked, "How would you like to take me upstairs for a quickie?" I looked at her and said "What are you nuts? I'm married." and left it at that. In hindsight, it was another trap to see if I would take her up on the offer. They all thought I was living with strippers in Arizona, which wasn't the case. Satan knew the truth but was filling everyone with all kinds of lies and ideas about me in an effort to build a case against me. To say I was living with strippers made me appear disloyal and since she always said that I was so superficial, it played in well with their concept of me. Satan, however, was always the one after the attention of any man that would give in to her. This conversation would come up over and over again throughout our lousy marriage. After all, this is the same woman that would dress up for a weekend to work with just the boss. Come on! I can only laugh now. Sometimes I wonder if I was really that naïve and stupid or just lacked interest; I don't know. In hindsight, everything always seems much more obvious and clear than when we are going through the motions of daily living.

Lesson One: It's not solely your fault

One sign to look out for is when your spouse constantly tells you that the marital problems are your fault and that you need to see a psychiatrist. Since I wanted to save the marriage for the sake of the boys, I had a few sessions with a psychiatrist in Arizona. I did inform Satan that I thought she should also see one since the family was nowhere close to being perfect; that would put her in another of her rages and she'd argue with me nonstop. During the psychiatric visits, Satan would then step it up a notch by saying that I needed to be placed on medication for "my" anger.

My brother, Mark, would pick me up from the airport and drive me home. As soon as I got in the door, the boys where there to greet me but Satan would start her usual bitching and then the verbal fighting would begin just about every time. I should have realized that this hell of a marriage was over long ago. I just wanted a wife and family to hug and love; someone that I could make happy and make me happy in return, instead, I came home to hell, after hours on the road, all alone, working my ass off. Traveling is very hard on the body and it's emotionally exhausting to have to deal with.

I remember talking very openly with the psychiatrist. In the end, the Psychiatrist in Arizona simply said that I was depressed but that there was nothing out of the ordinary wrong with me. When I told Satan he couldn't find anything wrong with me, aside from having a dysfunctional marriage, she would go into her usual rage because my behavior was relatively normal in the eyes of the psychiatrist. That Psychiatrist did place me on Zoloft for the depression, due to

Satan's insistence. **Be wary of taking unnecessary medication because it will come back and bite you in the ASS in court!** Since Satan didn't get the expected results, she began to complain that I needed to see a Therapist. She insisted that something was wrong with me and that therapy might help. Instead of saying no, I agreed to see one. My response to her was, "Sure Honey, anything to save this screwed up marriage." Of course, this is all part of her plan to set me up for the fall; just like when her best friend propositioned a quickie during the party and the lies she told about my living with strippers while working in Arizona AND HOW I WISH THAT WAS TRUE.

At this point, I'm taking Zoloft, seeing a psychiatrist and NOW a therapist. I was depressed over our miserable marriage but that was about it. I wasted sixteen lousy years in a loveless, sexless marriage!! After another argument, Satan decided she wanted to speak with my psychiatrist. She wasn't getting her desired results. **I stupidly signed the papers giving the psychiatrist permission to discuss my case with her; otherwise, HIPAA laws prohibit communication due to patient/doctor privileges.** She calls the psychiatrist to tell her side of the story, but he wouldn't bite. This again sends her into another rage. Satan tells everyone that I'm seeing a psychiatrist, therapist and taking Zoloft in order to play it up as if I was truly insane and had an anger problem. This would give her the excuse later on that she feared for her life and that of the children! Hang on tight, it's coming. This would also give her an excuse to obtain a restraining order, when the time was right, which was the first thing she did during the divorce process. Keep in mind that I never did anything to this woman in order for her to pursue one, BUT, **when a woman seeks the assistance of an attorney, she will provide her "poor me" version and make you appear like the villain.** Not to mention that her attorney is already on her side and will work with her to make you look as evil as possible.

Lesson Two: The Courts side with the accuser

Attorneys naturally have an agenda and have tried many similar cases so they know what works and doesn't work in court. They are familiar with the different Judges and what they stand for and what sets them off. Attorneys know what the Judge handling your case is bias against and so on. They will use that to their client's advantage. **If they truly hurt innocent people in the process, it's irrelevant and the truth does not always set you free.**

Her attorney will tell her that she will need to create a record on the soon-to-be-ex. She will need to take notes, call the police often to build a legal record and tell them that she fears for her life because he is a big bad man and he has threatened her or is capable of killing her and the children. You may think I came up with this assumption, however, one day when I was sitting in "my" attorney's office, waiting to speak with her, a woman came in and the paralegal gave the woman this similar advice. The Ohio courts can be very one-sided, so a man doesn't usually stand a chance. You are guilty and it's your job to prove your innocence. The police will be no friends of yours. **The attorney also told this woman that she had to act first because whoever begins and files the divorce has one up on the other party.** I couldn't believe what I was hearing because I was going through hell right now and they were helping this woman plot against her husband, which may or may not have been innocent of any wrong doing. Satan also had the advantage because she worked for attorney's most of her career and don't forget Mr. Legal Eagle in all this. You know the lawyer in Florida I talked about? Who, by the way, also happened to be a member of the Ohio Supreme Court, as well as a super attorney in South Florida! He was still around, just waiting to help bury me.

Also remember that Satan and her family have practically made a living in being the victims in order to take financial advantage of others and cover the many skeletons in their closets. That closet should have busted at the bolts long ago from all their lies and schemes. So not only are the courts on Satan's evil side, the police, Mr. Legal Eagle, her family and friends are now all plotting against me and now, even the neighbors were against me because of all her lies. Remember, I travelled constantly so I didn't have the time to socialize with anyone when I was home. That time was dedicated to my boys. Everything was in my face but I was just too stupid or naïve to realize it at the time. I just didn't think that people could be this evil. At this point, I want you to remember her sister's ex-husband and the stories they told about him liking weird sex, his mother bathing his 13 year old brother and the implied molestation of their children by the dad. Anyone see a pattern yet? No? Hold on, it's coming.

Lesson Three: Watch what you say and do

Satan always liked to think of herself as the prettiest woman alive and she demanded the best for herself. Before the separation, we were celebrating Christmas 2000. Everyone would be sitting around drinking and playing board games. My 2nd son, Jack, was playing with a new military toy knife Satan had bought him. Jack comes over and starts to act as if he's cutting my arm off because he liked to play war, so I played along. I play-fought with him and grabbed the toy knife away from him to pretend as if I was cutting his throat, which is how boys play-act in military games. Everyone was watching us play and, although no one said anything or reacted to this method of playing at the time, later, Satan made a big deal about it during one of the court hearings. During this time, in 2000, the IT industry was beginning to be outsourced to India. I began looking for other business opportunities that could not be outsourced, so I asked her brother in law, "Barney 5" who's a police officer, if he could provide some leads to help me get involved in crime scene cleanups since it makes well into the six figures and I wouldn't have to travel all over the country. Barney 5 was the guy her younger sister married after she divorced the first husband. They dated while her sister was still married to the first husband and working at the strip club. In turn, Barney 5 stated in the court documents that I wanted to learn how to kill and clean up a scene in order to eliminate my family. Since Barney 5 is a police officer, they took his statement as validation.

My brother, Mark, was also at that infamous Christmas 2000 party. He had no idea anything was about to hit me either! So after the game with Jack, I go over and sit on the couch and as I was watching the X-Men with the men. I made a comment about the blue woman, Mystique, saying "I would love to have her". This was then twisted and used in court by Satan to say that it was inappropriate talk around the boys, who weren't even in the room at this time, they were in the playroom. During the comment, the only ones in the room were the guys and one woman. I was not the only one that made that type of comment and even Barney 5 told my brother that he was getting free cable and watching porn, just like my father in law did years ago.

Be very careful because "your" comments will come back to bite you in the Ass. It's as if you need to walk around with a video camera for your own protection. I never got along with Barney 5, so he also knew what was going on well before I did.

So now, I'm seeing a Psychiatrist, a Therapist, taking Zoloft for depression, saying inappropriate things in front of the children who weren't even in the same room or hearing distance at the time and slicing my son's throat because I planned to kill them all and clean up the scene so I wouldn't get caught. How twisted is all that?!

The Beginning of the Divorce and Satan's Personal Cop:

The way I received word of my divorce went like this; I was in Arizona when I received a call from Satan, crying, to say; "I can't take the abuse anymore. We're getting divorced because I can't take it anymore." Then she disconnected the call before I had a chance to say anything or have her words register in my mind. I had no idea what she was talking about. At this point, I didn't even know that we were getting divorced or that there were any plans made, so I called her back to ask what the hell she was even talking about. She would just reply that I was harassing her and that if I didn't stop calling her, she'd call the cops. Then she'd hang up again. I called back for a 2nd time and Satan's fine Christian Deaconess mother picked up the phone and said it's between you two kids and I can't get involved." I replied to her by bringing up the Godly ways she, as a member of a church, is supposed to adhere to and mentioned marriage counseling. She had no reply to that. When her mother hung up, I called back again because I was still trying to obtain information and figure things out. This time, a police officer picks up the phone. By the way, this is the same police officer that would be at my house with Satan while I was away on business. He warns me that there's a TPO in effect against me. I asked him what the hell a TPO (Temporary Protective Order) was. He clarified and stated that if I get 600 yards from the house or contact her again, I would be arrested. I was in shock and said "But I haven't even done anything!" I was never even served until I showed up at a court hearing.

Lesson Four: Beware of rumors

From this point on, the SAME police officer showed up every time Satan had a complaint, whether it was day or night. When I picked up all the complaints at the police station, the same police officer had filed these reports on her behalf. During the court hearings, whenever this police officer appeared to testify, he would look at Satan with that stupid "knowing" look. I pointed out to my attorney that this same cop was the one that filed all the complaints, regardless of the time. She finally did something right and pointed this out to the judge by stating, "I didn't know she had her own private policeman." Of course, the judge did nothing about it.

The Temporary Protective Order came into play shortly before the snowstorm. In this TPO, Barney 5 (Satan's Brother in Law) stated that he had witnessed me with the toy knife; however, in the report he had stated that the knife was not a toy, but that I was acting as if I was cutting my son's throat with a "real" knife. I couldn't believe what I was reading. He also stated that I was under a doctor's prescription and seeing a psychiatrist and therapist. Now put two and two together.

My efforts to provide for my family also resulted in a conviction through their statements because I was never home and always on the road. Yes, I was making money for Satan to spend on herself and her boyfriends. She also stated that she wasn't sure if I had a weapon or not when she knew very well that I have never owned a weapon and have never had a problem with the police, but she needed to build a case and was being schooled by her attorney. Because she always liked to brag about her intelligence, I later found out that she had told her friends that she had planned this divorce for eight years. What kind of a woman but an evil, money-hungry woman would go to this extreme?

Beware of the rumors between friends, neighbors and her family members. You'll begin to realize things have been planned for awhile by this time. **So, again, act first to cover your ass and get a jump start on the process first**. Divorce is usually a war and not just a separation in the minds of these twisted women. They feel that they deserve everything, regardless of what you've done for them. They want to be done with you, however, they want you to work the rest of your life supporting them and the kids they had, whether they're yours or not.

I would have gladly handled things amicably with her, shared custody and even helped her out when she needed help if she would have done things the right way. A month after the separation, I was overwhelmed to be getting divorced from her and simply missed having the boys around.

At this point, I was virtually homeless and had no access to the tool of my trade. I was only allowed to pick up some personal items and nothing more.

Lesson Five: Keep your own tax records
Taxes and the IRS:

Satan calls me in Arizona BEFORE all this goes down and says "Oh, Honey we don't need to keep all these old tax records do we? We have never been audited before." I foolishly said "If you feel we don't need to keep seven years of tax records, let's get rid of them then." So she takes the old tax records and destroys them. Then in turn, her conspiring family calls the IRS and tells them I gave a false tax return for 1999. So during the divorce, I'm simultaneously dealing with the IRS. Satan had eliminated the tax records and since the TPO kept me from my own house and office, I couldn't retrieve anything without being arrested. She attempted to cry and filed twice for "Innocent spousal" with IRS, saying that she had no idea what her husband had done on the taxes. She was denied both times, but only because my tax attorney confirmed that she was the one that handled the taxes every year and every year had presented our tax attorney with paperwork in her own handwriting. He also had his own set of copies of my taxes.

If you're preparing for a divorce and things are not going well, keep separate copies of your tax returns, without the Soon-to-be-Ex, knowing a thing. Be certain to have copies of your tax records especially if you're self-employed or working on a 1099 tax form; it will help protect you since travel expenses, etc are all deductible but you better keep those receipts as proof, should IRS come after you. **The deductions will greatly reduce your gross income, which means that child support will be based on the**

lesser income most of the time. This is the reason Satan wanted me audited and at a greater income amount. She knew that if I couldn't prove the deductions, I would be forced to pay a higher amount in child support.

Lesson Six: Have separate bank accounts
Bank Accounts:

On January 2nd, while I was flying back to the jobsite and before I knew about the divorce, Satan had gone to our bank and closed all the joint accounts, re-opening them in a new account under her name only. A week prior to receiving the TPO my bank accounts had been closed. Over years of planning, Satan also had a bank deposit box where I highly suspect that all the money, over eight years, had been stashed away. I was aware that we had a safe deposit box but I never had time to look into the vault and see what was in it. I was too busy with the little time I was home handling chores and spending time with the boys and of course, fighting with Satan, so there just wasn't enough time to waste on visiting the bank and checking on the accounts. I had asked Satan why the hell we needed a bank deposit box and she would reply that our house records and other important boring paperwork needed to go in there for safe keeping. Needless to say, I'm eating out of a can, letting her handle the bills and accounts, which changed towards the end. That's when I decided to handle the bills myself because I was so upset that I was making $80.00 an hour, yet never had money for anything. I had my business credit card which was maxed out so I had to live with the two women in Arizona, who were a Godsend! To clarify, the bank deposit box was to hide money that could not be traced.

She would cry during the hearings "poor me; I have no money." This was believable to the courts since she was a housewife at the time, so the child support amount was reconsidered at a higher amount along with possible alimony; and with the readjusted tax return that was reported by her family after the records were lost, it's another beating on the wallet. Satan had such a history of being fired over the years and since I was making enough to cover the expenses, she had decided to stay home to supposedly raise the kids better. By the time the divorce was filed, she had been a Stay-At-Home mom for about 5 years or so.

During a divorce, Bank records will be demanded and if you're Soon-to-be-ex has a bank account it will show the amounts that are present; that doesn't mean there are no hidden funds though. Her parents' bank accounts may be used to deposit her money for safekeeping as well, pulling large sums of money from your account into theirs.

If you feel the marriage is not solid, **I would suggest that you have your own separate account and tell no one**, otherwise, you may find yourself homeless and penniless like I was.

The Private Investigator:

Satan had a P.I. watching me; I wasn't sure why, other than to keep tabs on what frozen garage floor I got to sleep on or what beach bench for that matter. No work, no money. She took me back to court just about every week for one reason or another. I would ask my attorney; "Aren't you supposed to be on the offense, because every time I turn around, Satan is?" My attorney's response was that it would take more money.

So aside from having difficulty finding work, how am I to keep work when something's available if I have court hearings every week; where I'm expected to shell out thousands of dollars to everyone and their brother? In essence, it wasn't very smart on Satan's part either because she had to spend her own share of money on her attorney, etc. and for what? Like I said before, after about a month of being separated, I was ecstatic about the divorce. I was finally going to be free of that witch. My only regret was the boys and what they would have to go through, which was the only reason I stayed married to her all those years to begin with, aside from just thinking that marriage was supposed to be that miserable in general. I knew that when I was out of the picture Satan would take her anger out on someone else and that would be one of the boys. She's always got to have a target. I even informed the courts of that, but they didn't listen.

Lesson Seven: Stash your stuff somewhere before it's gone Contempt Charges and Removing Items from the House. What a Joke!

This was a complete joke where Satan was concerned. She was in contempt so many times and the judge would simply warn her but nothing was ever done, however, **the first time they tell a man that he's in contempt, its jail time!!**

The first thing that the judge says is that no assets can leave the house without a court order, yet, she was able to move things over to her parents' house but I couldn't even take the computer I needed in order to continue working and make money. It was bad enough that business was slow due to the Y2K scare, now the Indian invasion (outsourcing) was on its way. There were very few contracts for American Consultants by this time and because I was locked out of my home office, due to the TPO, I was unable to obtain my messages for potential work. I wasn't allowed to contact her to even obtain my messages either. Yes, the courts are either not very smart or thrive on watching you fail because there is no way I was able to work effectively and still be expected to pay when I was denied access to my computer and all the information my home office held or my messages. I had to go to a public library just to be able to access emails to locate work, while I watched every dime leave from the sale of the house to pay for this divorce. It was approximately $350K. There was no money left by the time it was all said and done. Yes, I lost every dime but I gained my freedom, my life.

My advice to you is to begin taking whatever you want before it's too late. If you don't, you will likely not get another chance. Satan sold some of my things and even returned the Christmas items to the store in exchange for money. I even had one of those tall coke bottle banks that held the extra change that I would throw in there from all my travels. It must have been about $500.00. She cashed in the money. This is just a small example of all the things that she did right in front of the court, but when I had access to my own house, I couldn't take anything without being threatened with jail time for contempt.

Lesson Eight: Tell the Psychologist as little as possible Court Appointed Psychologist:

Approximately three months into the divorce proceedings, as if I hadn't gone through enough, the court appointed a psychologist. I had no choice but to comply because the courts are God and I had no say. Not only did I have to pay for this clown to speak with me, but for Satan's visits as well. I believe that these visits totaled around $5k. These visits also included every member of our families; our parents, siblings, etc.

Keep in mind that Satan is a planner so she had time to write a book on me in order to provide the Psychologist with what she wanted him to say in his report. I was unaware of certain going ons prior to speaking with him and wasn't aware that this was going to be a "show and tell" situation. At the time, I thought that we went in and just discussed what was on my mind pertaining to the relationship and the divorce. Where I went wrong was speaking about the lousy relationship and where I may have gone wrong during the marriage. **I would advise anyone that has to visit a court appointed Psychologist is to say NOTHING and just allow him/her to ask questions and give little to no answer.** Remember that you're charged by the hour and the longer you talk the more money you have to pay, just so that the courts can crucify you later on. This person is not there for you, but to report back to the courts. Make it short, sweet and simple.

This Psychologist would make personal phone calls to Satan. Anita, the children's' Guardian ad Litem, my attorney and I picked up on how he reacted to Satan when she was in the same room. It was pretty obvious that something was going on between Satan and this Psychologist. During the court hearing, the Psychologist pulls the report that Satan had written. It was almost word for word when it pertained to me. I couldn't believe it. I knew that Satan had provided him with the report because when I was able to have access to my home computer later on, I had recovered some of the documents that Satan and her sister thought they had destroyed.

Child Support:

When I was first hit with my child support payments, the judge ordered me to pay $10,000 a month. That was almost everything I had made per month, which was sucked up by the house payment, auto and living expenses, and the credit cards that I'd pay off, just so that she could rack them up again since she knew it would be her last big splurge.

I wasn't allowed to live in my own house and they wanted me to pay $10,000 a month in child support to boot, aside from all the expenses.

She cried to the judge by telling him that she sacrificed her life to become a housewife and stay-at-home mom in order for the children to have a proper upbringing, like she supposedly did, and now she had no skills to pursue a career. It now became my responsibility to prove that she was capable of finding a job. Since Satan had worked in law firms prior to having the kids, the judge denied alimony and required her to find work. VICTORY!!!

I had another friend who lived in California that was also going through a divorce. He also had an ex that expected him to make a six figure salary and wanted him to support her as well. Like Satan, she too was unfaithful and cheated on him the whole time. Never allow a woman to set financial standards before she decides that she's happy with you and your relationship. Further, **your salary and/or your potential to earn a living, in the eyes of the court have a lot to do with what will be awarded for child support and alimony.**

As I stated before, in 2000 the IT consulting business was being outsourced to India and similar countries. Since then it's become a greater issue in multiple industries as U.S. jobs are given away to non-U.S. employees. Jobs were beginning to become scarce for the American employees in my field. Add the divorce and IRS problems; gigs were hard to come by, however, the courts were ignorant to that fact and/or didn't care. Another thing to remember is that **when you begin making a specific amount of money, the court system doesn't believe that you will no longer have the potential to make that kind of money again**. Should the business falter and you have to enter another line of work, which is pretty much what happened to me, Child Support Enforcement will continue to use the old figures and say that you have the potential to make more, especially if you work on a 1099 rather than a W-2. They tend to have tunnel vision and become skeptical, so instead of using the last 3 years of taxes to determine a child support modification, they pull a "potential" higher figure to work from based on past income history.

The court system, Child Support Enforcement and Child Protection Services hide behind what is best for the kids and I do agree that supporting your kids is important, but not the way they look at things. In many cases, too much money is taken to support the children and now you have to obtain your own new set of bills, expenses and rent. I was lucky if I had enough left over to share a place with someone else or enough money for groceries when all is said and done. Oh, I'm just overjoyed to deal with this and now we have divorce rules, child support, IRS, and no money left to fight anything. The longer the case takes, the more money the attorneys and the court system make. **If you have assets and children, your court case can take years to resolve through continuations, like mine did. That's how the attorneys and the courts thrive.**

Visitation with the Kids:

If you are kicked out of your house, like I was, you will need to tell the courts that since the children are a priority and it would be in their best interest to have time with their father, it would be important to make sure visitation is set in order to have time to bond with them; but, how can you have visitation with them when you have no place to live? Satan didn't have this one figured out. Since I had the right to a weekend with them, the judge required Satan to leave the house for that weekend and allow me to move in. Needless to say, she was furious that she would have to leave the house for that weekend. Where she goes for the weekend was her problem. Who cares, IT'S WAR!! **Keep your focus on the kids welfare because they are the only good thing that will come out of this divorce and despite what anyone says, most will have psychological issues after this**. I have yet to see a child that was not affected by their parents divorce in some adverse way. Some just cope better than others.

The first time I picked up my boys was in front of my house. Daddy Dearest, their grandfather, had the gull to tell me that I would never see "our" boys ever again. I looked him in the eyes and said "When the fuck did these boys ever become yours?" That was the beginning of the Parental Alienation games.

On another occasion I showed up with my nephew, Jimmy, to stay at the house. Satan refused to leave, calling her lover, Mr. Legal Eagle. She attempted to bust through my arm and I said, "This is my time. You are out of here." So when she finally left, she called the police and reported that I physically assaulted her, which was false. The police never came by and never even spoke with me about the so-called incident, but it was another record. She also hired a security guard to stay outside the home and watch any movement that may transpire. What a waste of money and energy on her part!

When she returned to the house after my visitation, she filed another police report stating that I had disabled the alarm and that I had broken the window in the basement so that later on, I can return to the house and have a way to re-enter the house to harm the family. I told the police that they are welcome to look for fingerprints since I never touched the alarm system or entered the basement. Besides, if I really wanted to harm the family, I would have had ample opportunity long ago or this weekend for that matter. She sounded so ridiculous!

Another thing that happened during the exchange for visitation is that she would have her whole family outside to try and provoke me in order to secure another police report. It's all a game. I'll say it again; we could have had an amicable divorce, shared custody of the children, saved all those years of court battles and money wasted, because in the end, all the money was gone anyhow and there wasn't really much left to fight for. As the saying goes "You get more bees with honey." I would have been more willing to financially help her out throughout the years if she would have done things the right and fair way.

When I was informed by my attorney that I had a right to go by the police station and find out if there were any records filed, I was surprised to find out that mine were two inches thick because every time she got a bug up her ass, she'd file a complaint.

During one of my visits with the boys, I took them to my sister's house. Jack, my second son, fell and busted his tooth; when we returned, she filed charges against me with Child Protection Services for my lack of supervision. This along with other accusations began the start of supervised visitations.

A man interacting with the children can be very touchy and easy to misconstrue so be very careful. My children were young during the divorce so I would give the boys baths and that left the door open for her to claim child molestation accusations, like they did with her sister's ex-husband so many years before, knowing full well that these were false accusations. By the end of the divorce, we hadn't shared a bed for several years, so I would sleep in Jack's room since he had bunk beds. Jack would sleep on the top bunk while I slept on the bottom bunk. This again, became part of the molestation accusation.

Her intention was to damage my name in court so that she can appear like the innocent victim. All that the mother has to say is that she feels that you could have "done" something to the kids. **These accusations were thrown out due to lack of evidence, however, you are guilty until YOU can prove your innocence and even then, once there's implication and those words are uttered, you are looked upon with suspicion from that moment on**. Everyone begins to look at you as a monster and you will never regain that credibility in their eyes.

Everything you've ever said or possibly done will become twisted and used against you at this point. The children will be sent to a psychologist for that same period of time and you, not her, will be required to pay this added debt just because of these groundless accusations that were thrown out of court.

My family members were all attacked; my parents, brothers and sisters. Satan and her family had the time I didn't to prepare and plot their moves. In my case, my parents attend the same church as Satan's parents, so her parents spread rumors of child abuse and molestation throughout the church. For my parents, the church was and still is their life. In order to implicate me as a child molester, there had to be a pattern of how I supposedly became such a monster, which is why they inserted my parents into their twisted story. This way, they can destroy everyone simultaneously and still try to hide behind the bible to say what good people they are. This information came to our attention ONLY because the courts had sent my parents a letter outlining them as child molesters and abusers for the sake of a restraining order on them as well.

The other reason they did this was so I would have no place to visit with my kids. This family wanted to control my life, even after the divorce. Satan's father had told me the first day I got my kids that those kids were his and he was going to do everything he could so that I couldn't see them. What an asshole! But, be careful what you wish for; you might just get it and regret it.

The children were provided with a Guardian ad Litem, which is basically an attorney for the kids and guess who got to pay for this? Yep, you guessed it. Not the mother, but me. Again, more needless money out the window and more money for the court system. Not only do I get to pay for this attorney, but I get to pay for Satan's visitations with the children's attorney as well. What a deal!!! I was eventually required to have supervised visitations with the boys which required the presence of the Guardian ad Litem. Now every time I went to visit the kids, in the back of my mind, I thought "Shit, this is costing me $150 an hour." I also began to wonder how many hours Satan was racking up as well.

Satan was considered the victim so she could do anything with the kids but, I, as the non-custodial father, could not take them anywhere without permission because it may not be appropriate for the children. Everything I did was also reported back to the courts. By this time, emotions were up. Satan and her attorney were banking on my anger and frustration to get the better of me, this way the court system could persecute me further for my lack of helplessness because of all her deceit and plotting.

Be aware that once the molestation accusations are made and there is a court document to show suspicion and investigation, the doubt will always be there. Satan took that document to the boys' school. I would drop off my boys at school when I had them during visitation and the teachers faces would show their contempt, even though there was only an empty accusation which was later dismissed due to lack of evidence. My sister was a witness and she even over-heard them discussing the molestation document. I was so upset because there was no proof and everywhere I went, I was damned. Shortly after that, the principal escorted me out. This was very frustrating, emotional and draining because it was all false and out of my control. How does one prove that he's NOT a child molester? There was no evidence and the charges were dropped but that didn't matter.

Now I had reached my breaking point and had had it. It was time to move away and start a new life; otherwise, the court cases would consume my life. There would be no relief because everyone around me would just continue to bring up the case at every turn and that's not what I needed. I needed to get away for the sake of my own sanity. Staying and fighting, in my case, was doing me and the kids, no good.

I knew at this point that it would be better to give up fighting for the kids because I know how crazy Satan is and the courts were on her side for various reasons, none of which held any true or fair merit. To continue fighting would take an emotional toll on me and on the boys which were stuck in the middle of this war. I knew that she would never let me see the boys and she would simply use them for leverage against me. After the divorce, I did attempt to see my boys in December 2005 once again. After many attempts at calling and always getting her voicemail, she finally answered the phone and handed it to my oldest, Sam. In that particular conversation, I spoke with Sam and Jack. When I asked to speak with little Don, Jack stated that Don didn't want to speak with me because I wasn't his dad. When I asked him who told him this, he said, "Mom did." So Jack then handed Sam the phone who confirmed that same comment and then I finally spoke with little Don who said, "You're not my dad." Satan was preparing to move and disconnect that phone number because she was getting married to Beetle Bailey. This brings me to an email conversation we had months later where Beetle Bailey threatened me with physical harm and commented that my sons were "his" boys so that I should stay away and pay my child support. He also told me that she was the woman of his dreams. I made sure to warn him that he better watch his back and his bank account. Shortly after the marriage, he moved out and they were divorced about a year and a half later. Like I didn't see that coming!! Of course I did.

After that, I just kept tabs on the boys from afar until, I finally found Sam on Facebook.

Lesson Nine: Get a good attorney and don't be afraid to question them

I warn you, FIRST AND FOREMOST, MAKE SURE YOU HAVE A GOOD ATTORNEY that will fight for your interest rather than suck every dime out of you and not care what the outcome will be. I had a lousy attorney who was rarely prepared and dragged me down deeper, leaving me to the lions. All my attorney wanted to do was take my money.

One day, my attorney stated that I seemed disgusted with her. I told her that I was because we were never prepared and it was costing me a fortune. She did state that we could end it there. That should have clued me in but I thought we were almost at the end of this thing and just wanted a conclusion to this whole mess. My attorney also said that this could be done if I signed over everything to Satan which I refused to do. Basically, after two years of paying, she felt that she could not represent me anymore. I said that I was almost done and that she should see it to the end with all the money I blew on her to date. It took another year before a conclusion was finalized. I should have replaced my attorney long ago.

Never be afraid to question your attorney and if he or she is NOT doing what's in your best interest, do not be afraid to replace them IMMEDIATELY as I should have done years ago. You may even like your attorney as a person but that won't win the case if he or she is not representing you well.

My Best Friend, Les:

Les was one of those friends that one just doesn't forget. People either loved him or hated him. He loved to push people's buttons and could be a real asshole at times, but he was a lot of fun.

The church had softball tournaments, which were the <u>only</u> thing I loved to do in that church. We would drink and raise hell while playing softball. My brother, Stan, was always the designated driver since he didn't drink when he knew he had to drive; so we weren't completely stupid, just partially.

Of course, Satan and her royal (pain in the ass) family would bad mouth Les and his family behind their backs even though Satan was good friends with his daughter, Sally. Les pretty much disowned Sally because she was a lot like Satan. Satan would constantly bad mouth Les for having an affair before his marriage dissolved. Yes, Satan is obviously a hypocrite just like her dad. "Do as I say and not as I do." Her family felt that Les and his clan were beneath them, as if they were anything special themselves. As the years passed, I rarely saw Les or any of the guys that Satan didn't approve of. Either way, I was too busy working so the limited free home time I had was invested in spending time with my boys.

During the divorce, I began to reconnect with all my friends again. I'd fly back every week to see the boys, but Satan would always have excuses why I couldn't see them after spending time and money to fly in, so I'd go over to Les's and we would drink and talk. Les gave me a lot of advice and listened to me. He told me what was going to happen to me and the kids in this divorce. Les would tell me how much he detested Satan and her family; what a bunch of hypocrites and intolerant bunch of assholes they were. I had to agree completely. I just wished that people would have beaten me over the head with the truth earlier in the relationship, but I probably wouldn't have listened.

Lesson Ten: the "Five year plan".

During my first month of separation, Les sat me down in his apartment for the first time and we discussed what he called the 5 year plan. He said that if you're not the one that initiated the divorce and were caught off guard, then you're likely to fall into the 5 year plan. This means that the next 5 years of your life would be wasted with emotions of anger, depression and financial distress. At first, depression will set in because you're forced to start your life over and it's a difficult process to go through after having established yourself with a home and family. Next, the anger and hatred for your ex will set in and then finally, your finances will bottom out with help from the court system, attorneys, possible foreclosure and bankruptcy. I took Les's advice back with me to Florida and as I thought of his words, I thought to myself "Why the hell do I want to waste 5 years of my life over this?" I was 36 and had already wasted 16+ years with that woman. I wasn't going to spend another minute pining over it and was going to enjoy my freedom and celebrate a whole new life. Immediately after that, I began going out, enjoying the night clubs and South Florida parties. I was in love with the Florida night life. Another thing that Les told me was that the first woman I had sex with was going to be an "angry lay" so to speak. He used a more colorful word than "lay." Les said that after the first one, I'd go crazy and make up for all the years of celibacy I lived with Satan, screwing everything in sight. Let me just say that I enjoyed every minute. Satan had once told me that some woman might find me attractive. Let me just say that I've never had a problem and had many propositions that I turned down because I-WAS-MARRIED. The Florida women are "wow!" That's all I can say. They were nothing like the women in the Midwest. Many of them were up for anything and having fun. The diversity in cultures, beauty and behavior was refreshing. I was in paradise.

Les would tell me to forget the boys for now and walk away or things wouldn't go well and that one day the boys would come looking for me and then they would discover the truth. In the end, they would hate their mother for all she had done. I never believed him back then but as I write this book, I'm beginning to see these predictions made so long ago.

Les hadn't felt well for some time so he kept going to the doctor because something just didn't feel right. He was misdiagnosed for four years and then he was finally diagnosed with Pancreatic Cancer. By this time it was too late. Les knew his time was limited on this Earth. During his time, I paid for him to visit me in Florida. We partied and carried on the entire week he was here. I paid for everything and was happy to do so. I really didn't care if it left me broke. He was a great friend and he deserved it.

His cancer became worse. He died nine months later. Les and I would have long talks about his funeral. Les would say that he didn't want Satan and her family there.

Before his death, Les was admitted into a hospice. I would fly in to visit him. One day, Satan and her family had the gull to visit Les when I was there and since Satan already had a restraining order on me, I had to leave. As if she wasn't evil enough, her and her family had the audacity to make an appearance at Les' funeral so that I couldn't attend. Les hated her as much as she hated him, but that is the kind of twisted being that she is. I carry the good times and memories of our time together, which I cherish deeply. I talk about him regularly with friends and my beautiful wife, so it's as if he's still here with us. He wasn't perfect, but he was a good, down to earth person and an amazing friend. I recently spoke with his ex-wife. They had mended their relationship before he passed away and would have remarried if time was on their side. She tells everyone that he was the love of her life.

Lesson Eleven: Have a credit card in your name only and separate bank accounts Bankruptcy and Credit Cards:

Satan had cleaned out the joint bank accounts and left me with every possible bill imaginable. Then, while I was in Arizona, she went out on a spending spree right before I had any formal knowledge of the separation. She ran up every credit card we had because she didn't want any available credit accessible to me. Since she was a housewife, she knew the courts would likely make me pay for everything while she lived off of me until the divorce was finalized.

Since she had already preplanned on tapping out the joint credit cards, she obtained her own set under her name alone before our credit crashed, should I decide not to pay the joint ones off. I've learned that **it's always prudent to have a credit card in my name alone. During the divorce process, the credit card can become your lifeline** when all other liquid assets have been depleted or have become inaccessible.

Bankruptcy plays a role in many divorces. In my case, Satan took her half of the joint bills and filed for bankruptcy, which killed my credit score by 400 points. The bankruptcy was listed on my record even though I didn't file. Because I didn't file, however, creditors attempted to collect the unpaid balance from me. The way creditors locate a person is through phone records, utilities records and other cards under one's name, but in my case, I had nothing under my name so it became that much more difficult to be found. I obtained another credit card through my sister's credit as a "User." They could not track me under another's credit, even if I was listed as a user of their card because credit checks on users are not run. I made sure to pay it off every month and this helped my sister's credit improve. After several years, it didn't pay for me to pay off the old credit card debt because if I made a payment, then the time for my credit to become wiped clean would be extended rather than finally clearing out and beginning fresh, so it was not beneficial to make any payments. At this point in the game my business was ruined, I was expected to pay $2,500 in child support per month, along with all of her bills which totaled approximately $100,000. Then there were the past taxes I was being charged for by the IRS because she destroyed the $40,000 deductions so that my salary could appear higher and I would be charged more for child support. The only benefit to the taxes is that I could go after her for half after I paid it off since they denied her the "Innocent Spousal" credit twice, however, there's a deadline on how long I have to go after her from when I paid it off.

To date, I have not gone bankrupt. What I did after I met my wife was help her fix her credit and make sure that everything was under her name only. I own nothing. Although I've been divorced from Satan for many years, she still thinks that she is entitled to everything I own because we have children together and will harass Child Support Enforcement to charge me for more child support, so **keep it simple and under another's name after divorce**. Another thing to keep in mind is to never file taxes jointly with your current spouse or your spouse's salary and assets because that will also be included in your child support, giving the ex an opportunity to obtain more money she may or may not use for the children. Bank accounts should also be separate from that of your current spouse's for the same reason and in case you have arrears so that Child Support Enforcement would not be able to wipe out every penny the household has and give it to your ex. Child Support Enforcement WILL keep tabs on any assets and bank accounts under your name. They cleaned my bank account out twice. Every penny I had, so I ended up living on the street twice since I couldn't pay my rent when they wiped me out. They will think nothing of it as long as the child support is paid. If you own a home and are behind in child support, Child Support Enforcement will go as far as placing a lien on your home. Divorce is not the end when there are minor children involved. Again, I emphasize that it's important to help raise and financially support your kids but when the mother is uncooperative, she can keep the kids away and it would cost you time and money to take her to court, just so that she can get a slap on the wrist and once it blows over, keep them away again. However, miss payments and it doesn't cost her a penny for CSE to come after you. They will also state that one thing has nothing to do with the other, yet, don't pay and we'll see how prone the ex is to let you see the kids, if she allowed it in the first place. The court system has made it possible for the custodial mother to hold all the cards and create parental alienation. That's not to say that there aren't any deadbeat dads but many are not and are just fed up and placed in positions that they can't control. For every deadbeat dad out there, there's a malicious, malcontent and dysfunctional mom.

A new and happy beginning:

I met my current wife, Gina, during a contract. The contract only lasted two months but it's likely that the objective was to meet her and move on. She has been my support system and after all we've been through together over the years, I finally learned what the true definition of love and marriage really is. She's my partner and soul mate.

Gina introduced me to a good friend and coworker, Jerry, who happened to be a retired New York Attorney. Jerry became a great friend but, to us, he's family. He provided us with a lot of useful advice as to how to deal with the courts and Satan. Jerry, like many others, told me not to worry because the boys would come searching for me when they became older, at which time, the truth will be told.

Jerry is a very wise and honest man. He would say "**You always play fair, until someone breaks the rules and then, all bets are off.**" Words to live by. With his help, we began preparing goals, reviewing options and focusing on objectives for the future.

How I finally found my oldest son:

I found my 16 year old son, Sam, through Facebook in mid-February 2009. At least who I thought may be Sam, since there was no avatar picture or more information to confirm that it was my son, other than his name and the city he lived in. Two weeks later, he responded in a rather belligerent way, which I pretty much expected until I was able to explain my version. It was apparent that he had great dislike for his mother and grandparents (her parents) during the first discussions together. The emails continued with a variety of rude comments and criticism. I just let him vent until he calmed down and was able to hear me out. After all, I hadn't really been in his life for nine years so I wasn't going to begin reprimanding him about his behavior yet.

The first time, discussion over the internet didn't end well. Two days later I decided to send him a more detailed e-mail explaining that this had nothing to do with redemption, since he kept bringing up the word previously. It had more to do with my need to connect with him and provide him with my information should he need me and explain what had truly transpired over the years. He did respond and we were able to discuss a few things. At the end of the conversation via email, he didn't contact me again for days. I was thinking of sending him another email, however, my wife told me to allow Sam time to digest everything that had been discussed so far and to allow him time to contact me instead. Probably a month passed and I received a picture text on my cell phone with a note "Guess who?" Now we began texting back and forth. He was still rather resentful and rude but not as much as the first few times we communicated.

The contact became regular between us but still no phone calls; just text and emails. Much was discussed and resolved. His mother and grandparents had told him and his brothers that I had abandoned them, rather than how they kept me away and would call the police when I was supposed to show for regular scheduled visits. How she would make a point to not be there with the kids when I showed up for visits, even though I was flying from Florida to Ohio for just a few hours with them. I think that aside from everything he was already going through with his mother and how I described my life with her, which was pretty similar to his own, the timeline I gave him, showing that I had kept track of him and his brothers to the point that I would leave notes at his grandparents door, helped him realize it. During this discussion, which was finally over the phone, he stated "Oh so that's what they meant by me and notes." He had overheard his grandparents speaking about it but they never notified him that I was trying to get a hold of him. He put two and two together and realized what had really gone on.

I told Sam about the time I had my friend, Glen, drive down their grandparents' street. It was early, around 6:30am. My friend saw Daddy Dearest outside because Glen had almost accidentally run over the dog Satan had bought the boys when they were visiting me in Florida, which was our one and only visit. I had gotten word that the boys were being shuffled back to their grandparents' place once again. Every time she had a new man or wanted time for herself, she'd ship them off somewhere. Glen placed his cell phone on speaker and I typed the conversation word for word. Glen at 6:30 am drove back and forth on Hell Lane.

Glen sees someone after he almost ran his dog over.

Glen says do you know Daddy Dearest?

The man says "Maybe!" with a nervous tone. The man asked, "Do you live on this street?"

Glen says, "No."

The man says, "What are you doing?"

Glen says, "I'm investigating." And then replies "You're Daddy Dearest! Do you know me?"

Daddy Dearest says, "No. No I don't know you!" very nervously.

Glen then asks, "Does your grand kids live with you?"

Daddy Dearest says, "Yes, they did."

Glen says, "Does your kids go to this school district?"

Daddy Dearest nervously says, "No and I don't know where they are. Why are you asking?"

Glen says, "I'm an investigator. Private."

Daddy Dearest then says, "I'm not telling you anymore."

Glen says, "You have told me more than enough." Then he drives away.

The way phone conversations finally came to be was one day when Sam had text me about a car he was driving. His mother wanted to sell him the car for $900. The vehicle had over 180,000 miles on it and although Sam only had a summer job, she was capable of charging him but she would not give him the title to the vehicle. I told him that his Uncle Mark was a mechanic. He asked for the address which I provided him with. I told him to go see Uncle

Mark and whatever work the car needed, I would pay Mark for later. Sam, without his mother's knowledge, drove to my parent's house and met up with Mark. This would be the first time I would speak with Sam over the phone and from that day, we spoke everyday for approximately 3 hours each night. At least, until he got into an altercation with his mother, who had discovered early on that, we were communicating. She had not said anything, merely sent me an email with pictures of the boys, out of the blue. I suspected that she knew something because it wasn't like her to send me anything unless she wanted something. She also liked to show her intelligence by cluing me in with some hint; like the time that she told me that her married boss had a girlfriend. When I asked what she looked like, she stated that she was about 5'4" with dirty blonde hair. I didn't realize at the time that she was talking about herself.

After that day, Sam and I spoke every night. I finally decided that I needed to send him a cell phone because he was using the home phone and when she got the bill, if she didn't know by that time, she would then. Sam gave me a friend's address and I forwarded an extra cell phone I had available and told him to keep it private. My wife applied the numbers he would need to get a hold of us, which included his Uncle Mark's and my stepdaughter's cell numbers, just in case. She also decided to place a lock code on the phone so that only Sam could retrieve his contact list.

I obtained a fortune of information during our conversations. I was mostly interested in knowing about him and his brother since I had years of catching up to do. We discovered that we were very much alike. We enjoyed the same music, TV shows and appeared to have the same personality. His mother would come up in conversation when he'd state how much she hated the shows or music he would listen to and how she blamed me and Sam for everything that went wrong in her life. Satan would also tell him that he was just like his father and how she couldn't stand his father, on a regular basis. For those who think genetics doesn't play a deep role in one's personality, I can say that although I haven't spoken with Sam in years or seen him, he is not only the spitting image of me but carries many of the same personality traits, down to the way we type our sentences. In fact, when I mentioned that around our house, we call her Satan, he laughed and said that it was ironic because that's exactly what he calls her when he's with his friends. Basically, once we cleared the air and got rid of all the years of junk she bestowed on them about me, all the lies and deceit, we hit it off great. It was as if we'd been talking with each other forever.

Of course, now Sam carrying my DNA also has its setbacks. One is certainly my emotional Irish personality that hurt me in court so many times when I felt frustrated and trapped from all the lies. **We're honest and just say what's on our minds, which at trial is a big mistake.** The other setback is, well, my strong sexual nature, which became a problem because the night Sam got caught was the night Satan, out of character, was sniffing around. Sam had already caused more problems than usual. He had a bedroom in the basement, where the desktop computer was. She had already removed his door so he tacked up a sheet for privacy. He had intentions of sneaking out after our conversation as he did on occasions but I told him not to because if his mother was still downstairs at that time of night, then she knew something was up. He thought he was smarter than her, so when she went up for the night, out the window he flew. Needless to say, she discovered he was gone and called the police because she thought he was running away. The police caught him with a girlfriend and with his pants down. At this point, they took him in and he was required to call his mother from the cell phone I sent him. It was around 4am in the morning when he text me to tell me what was going on and that she was going to discover the cell phone. Not to contact him so the numbers could be safe. That's when things really heated up in that household. This particular night was later confirmed by my son Jack. He stated that Satan told the police that I was trying to kidnap Sam. Satan ran my picture to the police officer, while Sam sat in the police car. Satan told the officer I was trying to kidnap my son. Jack was right there and heard everything. This is how far this woman will take things just so I don't have contact with my boys. The funny thing is that I was in Florida, talking to the police the whole time this was going down so they likely realized what a nut she was, especially since they were always being called to that house over the years.

The following day, Satan's family went over to the house to interrogate him because they do things as a group. Evil never sleeps or acts alone. Since Sam refused to provide the lock code, his grandfather smashed the cell phone with a hammer, causing Sam to go into a rage. Sam had told them that the phone was his dad's and that they couldn't break it because it wasn't their property. After his Irish temper flared up, he picked up the house phone and called me. I told him not to worry about the phone and that I would eventually send him another. He then told me that Satan was standing there and asked if I wanted to speak with her. I told him that I had nothing to talk to her about. At that point, he yells at her with all the hate he could muster up and said "HE HATES YOU MORE THAN I HATE YOU!" Then I heard "click" and we were disconnected.

Prior to this coming down, we had already discussed her regular tactics of "I fear for my life", like she pulled with me so many years prior during the divorce process.

We had called the police shortly after the disconnection but Satan had already beaten us to the punch as she's prone to do. She always falls back on law enforcement to get her way; always twisting her story to make herself appear innocent of any wrong doings; always the victim. We left a message for the arresting officer that night, who eventually returned the call.

The arresting officer was very pleasant and stated that Sam wasn't arrested for domestic violence but for drug paraphernalia. He stated that he tried hard to speak with Sam and to avoid having him arrested because he didn't have enough to be arrested for, but that his mom insisted. We were told that Sam mentioned that he wanted to live with his father several times and that he did not appear to be in a happy environment, however, he doesn't know what happens behind closed doors. This officer appeared to be sympathetic and understanding. He agreed that boys like Sam do not get to where they are because they live in a happy, stable environment. The officer mentioned that Sam did provide his father's phone number as his one contact and that once he was processed in Juve in a couple of hours, we should hear from him.

We waited for that call most of the night but no call was forthcoming. Early the next morning, we called the Juvenile Detention Center where he was being held and they confirmed that he was there; however, they denied him the right to make his call because his mother told them that she had a "No Contact" order. Since they were uncertain, they chose to play it safe and disallow connection between us. His hearing was to be held that morning and at that time, the mother would have to show proof of the "No Contact" order. If none was provided, then should he return to the detention center, they would allow Sam to call me! Needless to say, I was unable to notify him that it would be in his best interest to request a court appointed attorney and therefore, his rights were ignored by the Magistrate while she sympathized with Satan, especially since Satan provided an early email between Sam and I where we both discussed our mutual dislike for his mother. Sam tried to tell the Magistrate that he wanted to live with his father but due to the email, the Magistrate felt that it would not be in his best interest to allow that due to the mutual hatred for Satan. So instead, she allowed Satan to take him home where she would try to cause Sam further misery and try to cause him to break his probation. He was not allowed to contact anyone that Satan deemed a bad influence, however, he was allowed to contact me from the home phone, where calls would be recorded, although it was against the divorce decree. He was to spend two weeks on house arrest and three months on probation, without the use of cell phones or internet service. During this time, however, I did receive communication on his well being. Satan was trying to provoke him daily so he could break his probation. She screamed, yelled and carried on as was her habit, even though she considered herself sophisticated and high-class.

I finally made contact with his probation officer who blatantly blamed me for NOT telling his mother that he was smoking pot. I attempted to tell this jackass with a badge that his mother was very well aware of his pot use long before I ever got wind and she didn't bother to do anything about it until she was able to use it as her ace. After about two weeks of waiting, he sent me a copy of the police report and conditions of his sentencing, which confirmed what my wife suspected; when Satan couldn't have him arrested for domestic violence, she pulled out a baggie with some marijuana, which Sam claims wasn't his. He did claim the pipe, which had some residue of marijuana in it, so on his mother's insistence, he was arrested for drug paraphernalia. This really comes back to the fact that he and I were in contact, since he told the officer that he couldn't stand that "fucking bitch" and that he wanted to live with his father in Florida.

There's no doubt that Sam was not completely innocent, however, when a mother fails to be a true mother, keeps the father away by hiding the children and playing all her games, constantly screaming at them, abusing them verbally, emotionally and at times, physically, leaving them to their own resources while she runs after some boyfriend and just blatantly ignores them; children, who are a product of their upbringing, will either push forward or regress into their own negativity. In this case, Sam felt trapped and took the latter approach.

During this time, I wasn't working and we were virtually broke due to the economy and all the outsourcing, so we didn't have any money to help him or fight Satan; we continued to try any free resource we could think of. I contacted his school's Guidance Counselor who didn't even realize that Sam was in any kind of trouble because his grades were excellent. I notified him of the problems Sam was having at home and what had transpired in the hopes that he would at least speak with Sam since he was likely to become a runaway or fall into deeper depression. The Guidance Counselor promised me that, although he couldn't do anything unless Sam requested help, he would call him in on Tuesday morning and speak with him. After his discussion with my son, Sam told the Guidance Counselor that he was in some trouble but preferred that he not tell his mother that he had spoken with him or his dad.

While Sam was on probation, with his mother trying to get him to break it at every turn, his friends ended up turning their backs on him but a friend did manage to pick up a few things for me that Sam had left at one of their houses for safe keeping, which included Don's hair and toothbrush so that I could try and have it tested in order to prove that he isn't my biological son. Although it would not stand in court, it would hopefully put doubt and allow for a legitimate test. Another thing that was added to the package was his mother's "Pure Romance" business card, showing how this fine, devout Christian mother had gone into business selling dildos and other sex toys. She even had some sex toys lying around the house which the boys discovered. How appropriate!! Sam later told me that if we would have been a day later in obtaining the samples, his mother would have discovered them since she went to the home of every one of his friends in order to pick up whatever items he was having them hold for him. As his probation stood, we had little to no communication over those 90 days. His probation officer notified him that he had a right to speak with me but only through the use of the house phone since Sam was restricted from using internet or cell phones during his probation period. He chose not to contact me since Satan had the bad habit of going against the divorce decree and recording these conversations.

The Ohio Court System and Child Support Enforcement (CSE):

My wife and I had a hearing in August 2009 in Ohio. Now here's the clincher and to show you how the courts work. I was out of work and no money was coming in so we made sure to contact Child Support Enforcement and notify them of our predicament. We were informed that since I had done so well in paying the child support over the last three and a half years that I was up for review to terminate the diversion program I was in and that I qualified for a Child Support modification. She instructed us on what to forward and advised that we would not have to show up for the modification hearing. We did as she suggested and faxed over a letter requesting a modification.

Sounds simple enough doesn't it? Well, later that month we received a letter demanding I appear before the Judge in reference to the "Termination of Diversion" hearing. My wife called twice and left messages that were not returned. On Monday she called again and was informed that I had to appear or have a warrant for my arrest. "What!!!" Since the hearing was on Wednesday, I immediately packed up and got in the car to drive 925 miles to Ohio for this last minute hearing. The day of the hearing, I discover that since I was behind three payments, although I had paid over $50k in three years, they were not going to terminate the diversion program but charge me with three counts of felony. One per child. I was allowed to return home until the following month where I had to return for sentencing since the judge decided that he wanted to review my case a little further. I discovered that Satan had called the Prosecutor every day during those three months I didn't pay so that he could have me arrested for 3-5 years. Instead the judge chose to make me a felon but disregard jail time. In this economy, as if finding a job wasn't impossible enough, try finding one with a felony on your record. So the courts want me to pay but they make it even that much more difficult to get hired. Genius! It sort of goes hand in hand with the courts expecting us to work, but require us to appear for court hearing after court hearing. Either they are very stupid or they really want us to fail. I'm thinking it's both. Very little the courts seem to do is logical but definitely directed towards more money in their pockets because that's all they were accomplishing with their decisions.

A Surprise Call:

A few weeks after our return home and not knowing which direction we were heading in life at this point with no jobs in the horizon and now a felony that was going to simply narrow down any options, my mother calls me from Ohio and says that my second son, Jack, had called her asking for my number. We found this very suspicious because not only did Jack call after years of no communication, but he called my mother's cell phone number which was not a known number to many. After discussing the situation, I remembered that Satan's parents called my parent's house a while back but my brother, Mark, not knowing who they were, gave them my mother's cell number.

Knowing how conniving that whole family is, we thought that maybe Satan and his grandparents set him up to this, otherwise, how else would a fourteen year old with a learning disability find this number? Jack had also apparently called from his home phone number but gave my mother his cell phone number for me to return the call. My wife suggested that it would be best for my mother to call Jack back with my cell phone number, that way if it was a trick, Satan couldn't say that I was harassing them like she did years before and have a reason to obtain a restraining order.

We also had a Child Support Reduction hearing coming up and whenever there's activity; Satan tends to appear in search of information, which gave us another reason to believe that this was a trick of some kind. Mom left Jack a voicemail on his cell but we didn't hear back from him until a week later.

We arrived for the child support hearing in Ohio and waited to see if Satan would appear, but no Satan. At this point, Satan was already dealing with quite a few issues in her life; foreclosure of her house, another divorce to a marriage that barely lasted but a minute, Sam who was still on probation, maybe Jack and unemployment unless she managed to get hired again along with the Child Support Modification, so it could have been a number of reasons why she didn't show up. There's never been a day that this woman didn't create drama in her life.

The magistrate called us in for our hearing and since Gina had everything lined out for him in a previous dispute letter to Child Support Enforcement along with evidence she had faxed. The magistrate merely went through the information we provided and with Satan absent, she was unable to contest it. You would think it was pretty much a slam dunk and that something finally resulted in our favor. We really weren't working and with the evidence of the state of the economy nationwide, it was rather clear what was going on. The Magistrate seemed to be understanding about outsourcing as I explained my situation as well. He had a copy of my taxes for the last three years that showed how little I had made and that the "Potential" amount child support enforcement kept using year after year, to keep my child support up was nonexistent. He reduced my salary to minimum wage and stated that this should substantially reduce my child support. In three weeks, we'd have the results.

After the hearing, we picked up our kids from my mother's house and drove home 925 miles. We just wanted to go home to Florida and not look back. We were finally happy that something had worked out in our direction since so much had gone wrong. I can officially say that 2009 has been our worst year together due to our economic situation. We had hit bottom.

Another thing about the whole court system and their archaic process, with technology today, why is it that they don't seem to know what's going on within their own division? One judge had no idea what the other judge had done or that I had even filed for Child Support Modification and had a hearing pending when the felony-happy judge had accused me of not requesting a modification. I, not only had to clue him in but I had to also clue the magistrate during the modification hearing of what that judge had charged me with. Which left the magistrate shaking his head and offering some "off the record" advice.

As we drove home, my cell phone rings and it was Jack! Jack was attending the Springer School for a disability and although he was just turning fourteen, he was a rather naïve and innocent fourteen year old. We talked as if we had never lost touch. He begins by saying "Dad, its Jack." And then he tells me that his mom wasn't home and he was talking outside so his brothers didn't know he was calling me. I asked him how he obtained my mother's number and he said that his grandmother (Satan's mom) picks him up from school so he sneaked her cell phone and found his other grandma's number in there, so he memorized it and then called her without their knowledge, because they would have been mad at him. He was calling from the house phone and he thought his mother wouldn't find out, although I knew that it would only be a matter of time before she discovered the calls. Jack mentioned that he had tried to get my number from his mom and grandparents for a year but they wouldn't give it to him. His mother told him that I was a bad man. I asked him why she said that and he stated that it was becasue I spanked him. I then said that I had spanked him but I bet his mom spanked him a lot more and his reply was "Oh yeaaahh!" He also commented on how mean his grandfather was because he would hit him and scream all the time. How his grandfather hated me and how I was going to sue him for busting the cell phone I gave Sam. All the years of his grandparents and mother trying to poison him against me were in vain. Jack relayed information as if saying "What a rainy day." He heard it but it really didn't seem to register in his mind for him to resent anyone.

A call from Satan:

Satan called me one Friday morning. November 20th 2009, in fact, it was also my daughter's birthday. My wife answered the phone and Satan asked for me. I never wanted to hear this woman's whiny voice again, so my wife told her to email me. Satan sounded upset and told her that it was about Sam so my wife urged me to speak with the demon. I had texted Sam the night before. He was at rehab with Satan since he had just gotten off probation the week prior. So when Satan told me that Sam had been arrested the previous night for Grand theft, I thought it was another game of hers. She had already attempted to have him arrested for supposedly stealing a car she was trying to sell him before and had given him permission to use on a regular basis, so I asked her if it was about the car in her driveway. She told me to stop being hateful. I told her that she's untruthful and so I couldn't trust her. She disconnected the conversation. When we returned from therapy, due to my accident, we emailed her and it was obvious that when Satan doesn't plan for an event, she is totally at a loss. Her parents seemed to have been done with Sam so she had no one to turn to but me apparently, so she gave me updates and we corresponded through email periodically with the latest information. Then one day she brought up the topic of the 3rd son, which I highly believe isn't mine and although she no longer denied the affairs, she persisted to try and make me believe that he was also mine. She agreed to another DNA test so long as it was approved through the court system. She always fell back on the court system because she likely knew there was little chance that they would allow another since one had already been established. My attorney had stated that it would be an uphill battle to have another one approved. Conveniently, the John Edwards admission was coming out around this time, where Edwards admitted to paying off someone to falsify paternity test results for his illegitimate daughter with Rielle Hunter. Anything is possible, especially when the true father holds a high position or is wealthy, as is the case with Satan's then-lover. She was also unaware that I had a sample of young Don's DNA, waiting to be tested, for our own personal knowledge. We were just waiting for money to be able and have it done. A DNA test is not cheap.

Child Support Modification hearing

After Jack and I had been texting and speaking back and forth for some time, Satan would interrogate Jack every night. We gave Jack our address and she immediately pulled up the house on the Internet which included pictures of our home. Satan immediately downloaded and printed those pictures and description. These are then submitted to the courts. **Keep your personal information to yourself.** One thing did backfire on Satan though. Jack called me all excited when he saw their pictures on the entertainment unit, in one of the photos. It helped re-enforce that I didn't forget them and that they were part of my life and family.

On the day of the modification hearing, my wife and I appeared for the hearing but Satan did not show. The hearing did proceed and magistrate reviewed my file. He decided to grant the reduction. He stated that we would receive the findings and conclusion within 3 weeks. A month and a half passed and still no report. We finally receive the conclusion, in our favor, but no sooner than we received that, we then receive a retraction because Satan had appealed the modification, which was supposedly submitted on time. I just can't win with the courts in Ohio. I felt crushed because I'm a felon now and I really have no job and no money. The mortgage payments were four months late. We had purchased a used car back in January because my car was very old and out of commission. That car would likely be repossessed soon. My wife's vehicle was the only vehicle that was being paid for by her parents. We sat and began to read the

2 inch thick evidence and documentation the courts sent as to why the reduction was rejected after they had approved it. The evidence was mostly based on my wife's information, which they couldn't rightfully use. There were speculations and false information as well. They had stated that my wife owned four houses worth 2.2 million dollars. If this was so, we would not be in this predicament and the arrearage would have been paid long ago. My wife looked up two of the addresses that were listed on the documents and was unable to locate them. Obviously, she didn't own them if they did exist. The home we lived in was a house she purchased prior to our marriage and the only other home she partially owned was the one her parents live in, which was done for inheritance purposes. Both of which had depreciated $100k each, due to the state of the real estate market. Satan's documentation was included along with the so-called investigation Child Support Enforcement did, stating that it was highly suspected that I was benefiting and living an opulent lifestyle through my wife. Another thing that CSE made a big deal about was my wife's business, which we had told my probation officer about months earlier, when he asked. CSE stated that since my wife was a minority business woman, they suspected that she was receiving government grants for the business. The one thing you must know is that although those grants are out there, business will not come easy unless there's a big name backing the minority business up, which my wife did not have, so the business was a business in name only. There were no contracts, no business and no money at this time. All the business was being outsourced to India and China during this time in history. My wife, shortly, began studying and training for a career in real estate since there was no business in any other market and as many employment applications she filled out, there were no prospects or calls. The real estate market was beginning to slowly improve and it was something she wanted to do for many years.

This brings me back to the day of my potential felony hearing with Judge All-Knowing months earlier. As I stated earlier, I clearly recount standing there listening to him accuse me of failing to notify CSE about requesting a Child Support Modification, which we had indeed done months prior to the sentencing. Not only that, we kept CSE informed of our situation. The judge also commented that I made a lot of money. I responded by saying that I did prior toY2K. I also stated that I accepted the guilty plea only because I didn't have an option unless I wanted to spend a fortune I didn't have to defend myself and drag on court hearing after court hearing. I was told that if I pleaded "not guilty" and lost, the diversion program would be off the table and I could spend 3 years in prison. This was their way of forcing the Diversion program because as my attorney had stated, they didn't want this to go to trial. My attorney then stated that I should plead Nolo Contendre, which placed me in the Diversion Program. Nolo Contendre (No Contest) is another word for guilty. It was the only true option I had due to time and money. This was 3 years prior to my sentencing, where he clearly saw that I had paid over $50k in those 3 years. By the way, how I even got into this program is because I was Paying Flordia CSE, who in return was supposed to pay Ohio CSE, but instead six months worth of payments ended up in tthe Abyss to be recovered later.

In 2009 and unaware of where this Judge was going with that BS, he had said that he was going to order an investigation and then make his decision. **BEWARE of those investigations.** Whatever moron performed mine was obviously bias and failed to provide facts, yet, it was still taken into consideration while they danced around their speculations rather than being up front and asking me for clarification, which we would have gladly provided. The judge's questions didn't become clear until I received the so-called findings and court documentation retracting the already approved reduction. This just shows that they can do whatever the hell they want.

While the Judge awaited the conclusion of the CSE investigation, he sent me to see the dumb asses in CSE before I was to leave Ohio. You should have seen the looks on their faces when I was trying to explain my position and lack of work due to the economy. They were attempting to use the same salary that was used in 2003, which no longer existed. It was obvious that these morons didn't believe a damn thing I was saying despite the nationwide hardships, due to the economy. The CSE Caseworker was pissed when they asked whether my wife and I filed taxes together and I said that we filed separately. They don't like this a bit because they would just love to be up my ass, in order to take everything like they had done twice before when they cleared my bank accounts and left me homeless, which was before I met my wife. Now the stakes were way higher since my wife had a house, however, the house was purchased by her prior to our marriage and I'm not on the deed, so CSE could not place a lien against it. I simply left frustrated since they were unhelpful and trying to make it as impossible to assist me as they possibly could.

My wife and I appeared the following month for the sentencing. The Judge decided that I would not serve any jail time but based on the "investigation" he charged me with 3 counts of felony; one per child. I was then released and ordered to see my probation officer, which was the ONLY person that asked us about the corporation under my wife's name. I looked at my wife and she answered him immediately. Nothing further was asked. By the way, he was the only one that listened to her. No judge or the magistrate wanted to hear anything my wife had to say, yet, they seemed to be ok about using her information to prosecute me. I can not emphasize this enough!! If you get into a situation where you have a probation officer, GET ALONG WITH THEM! They can either help you or have you prosecuted. Yes, they can be a pain in your ass with restrictions but they can make it easy or very hard! After my initial meeting with mine and they realized what a warped case this was, my P.O.s did an about face and treated me nicely. I had one in each state but only really had to report to the one in Florida; however, I kept the one in Ohio appraised on everything. They both helped me within their limits and certain things were said that clued me in on my possibilities after probation was over, which were actually very promising. It was just a very difficult time in my life because I had no money and was unemployed for over a year but tried to make the best of it with my wife and kids. We learned to pull the positive out of such a difficult and negative situation.

Since the modification and the felony, I was almost run over by a truck while I was on my bicycle. I was going down a hill and a truck, which was originally at a stop sign, turned left, coming straight up the middle of the road towards me and my wife. I was behind her and pinned between a parked vehicle and the truck coming at me. I slammed on both brakes to avoid the collision and went head over heels, landing on my head. The only thing that saved me was that I had a helmet on. I was transported to the hospital on two different occasions that night and diagnosed with a concussion, separated shoulder and bulging disk in my neck. My stomach that had been operated in 2006, due to a near-death car crash, had become aggravated once again. Although I didn't work after the first 2006 accident, due to my bed rest and injuries, we continued to pay the child support regularly. I had decided not to go on disability then because I had to work in order to pay the child support and make good on the diversion program, so I forced myself out of bed early and began working. Judge All-knowing, however, said that I should have gone on disability in 2006 because even with evidence of my injuries, pictures and dedication to keep up on the child support payments, it was NOW not enough. I tried to do my best and to the detriment of my health, disregarded it to go back to work and make good by the courts and the boys for nothing. Now, the courts don't like the fact that I'm hurt yet again. They don't believe I'm hurt at all and I had to prove it continuously because in the long run, it all goes against raising my child support, if I could prove that I was injured and disabled.

I was placed on probation until the arrearage is brought current which requires me to see a probation officer once a month and pay another $3,000.00 for this wonderful service.

So now we come back to the false report where my wife supposedly owns 4 houses worth 2.2 million. The business website, which helped them determine that her minority owned company, was receiving government grants, which I was benefiting from. She did try to obtain government work but after 5 years of trying, through RFPs and getting nowhere, we discovered that a big company had to be backing us up in order to truly win a bid, which wasn't the case. When the Judge read this report that this investigator presented, stating that they highly suspected we were hiding behind the corporation, everything became clear. I was judged before I even knew what the hell was really happening. They didn't even have the decency to confront me about anything in order to clarify any misunderstandings or provide proof. They also had the gull to convict me on portions of my wife's information but refused to ever listen to her during the court hearings. Once again, the father is guilty and the poor mother is the victim.

After receiving this 2 inch thick book of accusations, assumptions and presumptions, my wife wrote Judge All-Knowing a letter clarifying some of the falsehoods and even though she was not required to do so, she faxed it to his office with a copy of her personal monthly statement and the corporation's, which showed a whopping $34.00, approximately. Yep, that's a productive corporation all right. Maybe I can pay the $20k arrearage with that $34.00 and wipe the debt clean. As serious and frustrating as this all is, they are a true joke. **Don't be afraid to contest any falsehoods and set the record straight.**

Shortly after my wife submitted the correct information, another letter arrives stating that they had reviewed the documents once again and had determined that although Satan had filed in a timely manner, she did not file in a properly fashion. My child support modification was reduced along with the arrearage I was required to pay monthly by approximately $700.00. That's great however, when there's no money coming in to pay utilities, how am I supposed to pay the required child support with a felony record, which is holding me back from being hired anywhere and in THIS economy? Yes, they are geniuses, charging a father who's trying and has paid over $50k in 3 years, has chosen not to go on disability in order to work and provide, as a felon so that he CAN NOT find work but is expected to pay none-the-less. Our court system really works but the question is for whom?

The saga continues...

PRE-DIVORCE & SEPARATION PREPARATION CHECKLIST

Here's a list to help you determine what you should do, especially if you feel that your spouse is going to make the process difficult.

- Cancel all joint credit cards and clean out all joint bank and investment accounts. Immediately hit any safe deposit box you may have. She may have already been storing funds and valuables, in anticipation of a divorce. You may wish to obtain a PO Box before you move out of the house as a method of receiving mail. Law doesn't allow you to obtain a PO Box without a home address that can be traced, so do it now.

- Collect or make copies of all bank statements, cancelled checks, utility bills, insurance policies, copies of phone or cell records detailed that includes text messages, copy all computer documents users & hers, tax records with evidence of deductions, such as receipts, etc. for safe-keeping. Anything of value that she may be able to profit from should be in your possession. This includes guns, jewelry, personal effects that she can sell. Deny her control of anything she can hold over your head. Keep in mind that anything left behind, is hers.

- Secure any photos that have meaning to you, etc or you will never see them again. Don't forget to take and create any home movies showing you and your kids playing together. Place them in safe storage facility away from the principal residence.

- Secure your spouse's empty pill bottles and any mental records. NEVER submit to a mental evaluation she may request or allow her access to your doctor, therapist or psychiatrist. You are protected through HIPAA law unless you sign away your rights and give her authorization.

- Find an available place to live but do not move in. Do begin packing and storing away items. Including food, clothes, essentials, kitchen items, such as pots and pans, etc. Home décor, furniture and other important items to you.

- Contact an experienced attorney. Preferably one that specializes in Father's Rights, custody and divorce cases. File first. The person, who does, usually has the upper hand. Keep in mind that if the attorney isn't working for you fire that attorney and find another immediately. They do not all look out for their client's best interest, regardless, of how much he/she is costing you.

- Be a doting parent and continue to be involved in your kids' lives. Be sure to appear for PTA meetings, meet with their teachers, appear for games, etc. The more active you are and others see you, the better. Help them with homework and school work.

- Continue to provide for your children but keep receipts, check copies and all other evidence of purchases and payments. Buy diapers, meals, clothes, etc. NEVER give your spouse cash since it cannot be traced.

- Start preparing a list of witnesses that may have observed your good character and your spouse's bad behavior, if any. If you can obtain letters from these witnesses, do so.

- Avoid moving out of the home where the kids reside unless you are ordered to do so by a judge. Don't move out, not even temporarily, otherwise, she takes control.

- Obtain a copy of your spouse's resume and tax records to prove that she is capable of working and providing for herself. This can help cut out any possible alimony she requests, even if she has not worked in a while.

- DO NOT PUBLICLY EXPOSE ANY NEW GIRLFRIENDS OR INTRODUCE ANY TO THE CHILDREN until the divorce is final. That way you cannot be viewed as irresponsible nor have charges of infidelity thrown at you. The least evidence against you, the smoother the case will go for you. Spend quality time with the kids. You'll have plenty of time to date later. Remember that in most states, the law requires that the children have their own bedroom when visiting you, so be sure to find a place that has more than one bedroom.

- Document everything. Keep a chronological record of events, purchases, etc. Be careful what you write when emailing your spouse. NEVER THREATEN VIOLENCE. NEVER USE VERBAL, PHYSICAL OR MENTAL ABUSE. Be as civil with her as possible. BITE YOUR TONGUE. The more vindictive and out of control she becomes, the better for you. Keep calm.

- Be very careful that she may use the nuclear option of child molestation against you. Even if this is thrown out of court later due to lack of evidence, you may be required to have supervised visitations with the Guardian ad litem which represents the children's interest but you will be required to pay for their time. This will be hard to overcome because people will be doubtful and the courts will persist in bringing up the possibility.

- During your weekend visits and overnight stays with the kids, the spouse will attempt to control the situation with constant phone calls and later, interrogate them to obtain evidence against you. Be sure they sleep in a separate room from you, regardless of your relationship with them, to avoid the Nuclear Option charge. Be sure to have your attorney stipulate the maximum number of calls she can make while they are visiting with you. Any and all communication should be email so that she is unable to twist any verbal discussions between, however, be careful what you write so that it cannot be taken out of context. **Keep this in mind, after the divorce or final separation, as well.**

- You have a right to go to the police station, check and obtain any reports written against you by your spouse that you may not be aware of.

POST- SEPARATION/DIVORCE LIST

- Appear for all scheduled visitations and if she fails to allow the visit or is conveniently not home or unavailable for your visits, document this and the reason you were unable to see the kids. Document your expenses for these missed visits. Keep the receipts and all evidence. This will be a form of Parental Alienation or control. Carry an original copy of the custody or divorce decree that specifies your visitation time. This can help should you call the police for assistance. Be sure to notify her, in advance, that you will be visiting so that she doesn't have the excuse that she forgot or was unaware.

- If you have scheduled drop offs, make sure they are done in neutral territory and, if possible, take a witness with you. Preferably a non-family member. Do be aware that she may call the police so they can be waiting undercover with the precedence that she "fears for her life." The "life fearing" tactic is very common since women are viewed as the weaker and more vulnerable sex.

- Inform your supervisor or job officials that you are going through a nasty divorce and she may try to contact your work to create problems for you to have you fired. If she doesn't know where you work, keep it that way.

Just provide her with a home phone number or a cell number, at best. Try to avoid providing her with an address, if possible, but some courts may demand that the mother be aware of where the children will be living when they're with you.

- If by chance, you end up in arrears, CSE can and will withdraw your funds from your bank accounts, without your permission or knowledge. They can place a lien on any assets under your name, such as a home. They can demand you turn over your vehicle or sell it in order to pay arrears. That it's your only means of transportation is meaningless to them, even if it prevents you from going to work.

- Avoid any unsecure Facebook or business sites that you cannot make completely private to the public. Otherwise, she will be able to secure information about you as evidence to strengthen any future cases. She can also obtain a list of your friends and colleagues to try and ruin your reputation. Be careful she doesn't try to backdoor your through a mutual friend.

- Do not introduce a girlfriend to any of your kids unless you are certain that it will be a long term or serious relationship. The fewer women they are exposed to; the better for the kids.

- Try to keep their life with you as stable as possible. Too many moves, girlfriends and other constant changes can be construed as an unhealthy environment for them.

- Try to be civil with their mother in the child's presence and avoid any negative discussions about their mother with them. Especially if they are young. No matter what happens, it's their mother and that won't change.

As they become older, they will become aware of any wrong doing to keep you away from them on their mother's part and this can place a wedge between them and their mother. Just keep all evidence to show them later, if necessary.

- Just because you're divorced, doesn't mean it's over when there are children involved. Any raises you receive or changes in salary will be taken into consideration by CSE for modification purposes. What she does with the money, as the custodial parent, is not a concern they have most of the time, unless there's a reason that the money isn't being used for the child's benefit which includes payments of rents, utility bills, food, clothing, etc. If the mother has an addiction, such as drugs, alcohol, etc. and you can prove that the children's money is being used for unlawful purposes, this can be used against her. This can also help in possibly obtaining custody as well.

THESE ARE SUGGESTIONS BASED ON MY EXPERIENCES WHICH CAN BE TAKEN INTO CONSIDERATION BUT SHOULD BE REVIEWED WITH YOUR ATTORNEY.